EDUCATION

IN

RELIGION AND MORALS

BY

GEORGE ALBERT COE, Ph. D.

JOHN EVANS PROFESSOR OF MORAL AND INTELLECTUAL
PHILOSOPHY IN NORTHWESTERN UNIVERSITY

AUTHOR OF "THE SPIRITUAL LIFE" AND "THE RELIGION
OF A MATURE MIND"

CHICAGO   NEW YORK   TORONTO
FLEMING H. REVELL COMPANY
LONDON AND EDINBURGH
1911

CHICAGO: 63 WASHINGTON STREET
NEW YORK: 158 FIFTH AVENUE
TORONTO: 27 RICHMOND STREET, W.
LONDON: 21 PATERNOSTER SQUARE
EDINBURGH: 30 ST. MARY STREET

CONTENTS.

PREFACE

The present place of religious and moral education in our civilisation is paradoxical. Everybody knows that the moral health of society and the progress of religion depend largely, if not chiefly, upon the training of the young in matters that pertain to character, yet no other part of education receives so little specific attention. The growth of popular government has increased the importance of high character in the people, yet no substitute has been found, one has scarcely been sought, for the dogmatic religious instruction that has been properly excluded from the people's schools. At a time when the massing of the people in cities is exposing children as never before to the forces of evil, family training in religion and morals suffers, according to all accounts, a decline. At the bloom period of the Sunday school, complaints arise that the populace is ignorant, perhaps growingly so, of the Bible, and that the rate of accessions to the churches is decreasing. The age of reform in education, when we fancy that the child is at last coming to his own, is an age that neglects the most important end of education, and stands perplexed as to the means to this end.

We are, in fact, confronted by an emergency in respect to education in morals and religion. The emergency is not due, however, to poverty of resources. In the state school and the Sunday school we have two vast organisations which we may bring, whenever we will, under the more complete control of the highest educational principles. The nineteenth century made extraordinary progress in respect to the methods of teaching, and the results are ready to be utilised in church and home and school. Modern psychology, especially the child-study movement, is accumulating knowledge that has important applications to religious and moral culture. The store of biblical knowledge and of knowledge of religion is increasing, and it demands to be spread abroad.

To help bring this supply into closer touch with the need is the aim of this book. It is not chiefly a book of methods, nor is it merely a treatise on educational theory. It is rather an effort to bring the broadest philosophy of education into the closest relation to practice; to show how principles lead directly to methods, and so to strike the golden mean between unpractical theorising and mere routine. I have tried, likewise, to exhibit the principles and forces of religious and moral education in their highest concreteness as factors in the general movement of human life. A large part of our present difficulty lies just in the fact that our philosophy of life has been isolated from practical methods of training for life, and that this training has been isolated from the actual life of the world.

I have made no attempt to separate the religious from the moral factors in education, for the simple reason that they belong together in practice. Morals are not religion, and religion is not morals; nevertheless full-grown religion includes morals. The standpoint of Christianity, moreover, is that of wholeness of life, from which no human good can be excluded.

The division of the book into relatively short chapters, and of the chapters into numbered sections will, it is hoped, help to adapt the whole to the use of classes for teacher-training without detracting from the comfort of the general reader. Readers who desire to pursue further any of the topics herein discussed will find information as to reading in the classified bibliography that is appended to the work.

GEORGE ALBERT COE.

Evanston, Illinois, September, 1904.

PART I
THE THEORY

CHAPTER I

THE PLACE OF CHARACTER IN EDUCATION

1. Three Factors in the Idea of Education. What makes s c h o o l s necessary, and what are they for? These questions can be answered by a simple analysis of facts with which everyone is familiar. Schools exist, in the first place, because children exist, that is, because the race includes individuals who are incomplete but capable of developing. In the second place, schools exist because there are higher and lower kinds of mature life. Children are schooled *for* something. A conception of a goal, or a kind of life that is really worth living, presides, explicitly or implicitly, over all educational effort. Finally, schools exist because adults possess accumulated results of experience as to what is the better and what the less good life. Education gives to children the benefit of experience other than their own, and in advance of their own. Thus the factors involved in the idea of education are these: An immature being, a goal or destiny for life, and older human beings who can help the younger to realize this goal or destiny.

2. Over-Emphasis upon the Adult Point of View. Each of these factors has been at some time so prominent in the minds of men as to obscure one or both of the others. Up to comparatively recent times, the value of adult experience has so occupied the thoughts of educators as to prevent them from seeing the necessity of understanding childhood. Adult interests, ways of looking at things, rules of conduct, were assumed as a standard for all, and the school accordingly aimed to produce conformity more than it aimed to secure development. "Modern" education is based, first of all, upon recognition of the child as one of the determining factors. The differences between the child mind and the adult mind are noted, and the whole notion of education has become an application of the notion of development.

3. Over-Emphasis upon the Goal. Over-emphasis upon the goal or destiny of man is a general characteristic of mediæval education. The school was a handmaid of the church, and the church conceived her mission to men as that of saving their souls from eternal perdition. A religion broad enough to include

everything that is worthy of being a part of
our temporal life, and a religious education
equally broad, were not characteristic of the
period. The mediæval view of religion was
exclusive rather than inclusive; it contrasted
the goods of religion with the goods of this
world, the blessings of eternal salvation with
the fleeting things of time; and as a result
it could not utilise in education the whole of
accumulated experience, but only a part of
it. The educator was the priest—not the
man within the priest, but the priest as rep-
resenting the goal of life abstracted from
the content of life. For the same reason
the point of view of the child himself was
ignored, and the way was left open for repression and forced conformity as distinguished from development.

4. Over-Emphasis   At the present time this
upon the Child.   tendency is no longer
dominant. Education has been brought close
to the life that now is, so close, in fact, that
we sometimes forget to ask what this life
really signifies, what its goal is. Moreover,
another temptation to forget what the child
is to be educated for, grows out of the extraordinary emphasis that modern education
places upon the child himself. The laws of

the child-mind yield laws for educating that mind. We are not to conform the child to adult points of view, but the teacher is to conform himself to the point of view of the pupil. As Froebel says, ''Education and instruction should from the first be passive, observant, protective, rather than prescribing, determining, interfering.'' [1] From too exclusive attention to this principle, modern education (though not Froebel) tends to forget its own goal. It looks backward to the laws and forces of the child's mind, rather than forward to the destiny that is to be achieved. Nevertheless education is *for* something. It is development, but development toward something as well as away from something.[2]

5. The Aim of Education. Is it knowledge?   What, then, is the goal of education?

Most persons, if asked what the child is supposed to receive from the educational process, would reply that he receives instruction, knowledge, intellectual training. The success of a school

[1] W. H. Herford: The Students' Froebel. Boston, 1894, p. 5.

[2] ''It is the danger of the 'new education' that it regards the child's present powers and interests as something finally significant in themselves.''—John Dewey: The Child and the Curriculum (Chicago, 1902), page 20.

is popularly measured by the rapidity
with which its pupils appear to increase their stock of learning. This notion
arises in our minds in a natural way, for it
is a result of a long historical process, and—
we may add—of an ancient error. Man has
been defined as a rational animal, and his
moral and spiritual life have been supposed
to rest upon and grow out of a set of ideas
either reasoned out or believed in. Knowledge and intellectual culture were therefore
regarded as the essential marks of an educated man. We shall have occasion in other
chapters to discuss the relation of knowing
and doing. Here it is sufficient to note
merely that the intellectualistic notion of man
has been abandoned by the thought of our
time, or rather set into relation to the com-
plementary truth that man is will as well as
intellect. A corresponding change is taking
place in our notions of education.

6. Is it Power?   With the enlarging control over nature, and the
vast expansion of commerce and industry that
have followed the triumphs of modern science and invention, there has arisen a demand for men who can do things—men who
can build railroads and steamships, manage

vast properties, organise and lead men.
Under the influence of these practical demands, the populace has tended to modify
its conception of the aim of education in the
direction of power and effectiveness as distinguished from both learning and mental
acuteness. Instead of the "clear, cold, logic-
engine" which mere intellectualism regards
as the proper product of education, the drift
of popular thought is now toward another
kind of mental engine, the kind that keeps the
practical machinery of life in motion. But
we cannot stop here. For modern commerce
and industry are not more distinguished by
a new relation of man to things than they
are by a new relation of man to man. The
relations between men are becoming wider
and more complex; there is greater depend-
ence of one upon another; and just at this
juncture the modern city springs up to teach
us that we are still in the rudiments of the
art of living together. Meanwhile the experiment in popular government is seen to
depend for its outcome upon the kind of character that prevails among the people.

7. Is it Social   These   conditions   are
Adjustment?   forcing   upon   thoughtful
men a conviction that the great need of our

time is a full-grown, wisely directed social consciousness, and that the development thereof must be the aim of education. The school is an instrument of society for social ends. It must not merely train the intellect, impart knowledge, and develop power; it must also fit the individual for occupying his proper place in the social whole. The day is already past when an intelligent educator can think that his work consists in training or instructing individuals as such. Of course education is training of individuals, and more attention than ever is being paid to individuality, but the final consideration is not the individual taken by himself, but filling the proper place of an individual in society. This implies respect for the rights and interests of one's fellows, readiness to co-operate for common ends, and a sense of political responsibility. Thus the end of true education is seen to fall within, not outside of, the sphere of ethics.

8. Education is Ethical in both End and Process. That education aims not at mere knowledge or mere power of any kind, but rather at knowledge and power put to right uses is fully recognized by the educational thought, though not by the popular opinion, of the day.[1] The advance movement in religious education takes its start, not in an educational atmosphere that is indifferent to the higher values of life, but in one that is already suffused with moral aspiration. Here and there, no doubt, a teacher entertains a contrary ideal of his work; probably the number of teachers who have not awakened to serious reflection upon the nature of their work is considerable; but certainly the general mass of those who do reflect will be found by any

[1] Witness the following typical definitions and propositions:

Nicholas Murray Butler: "Education is 'a gradual adjustment to the spiritual possessions of the race.''—The Meaning of Education (New York, 1898), page 17.

J. G. Compayré: Education is "the sum of the reflective efforts by which we aid nature in the development of the physical, intellectual, and moral faculties of man, in view of his perfection, his happiness, and his social destination.''—Lectures on Pedagogy (Boston, 1893), pages 12f.

William James: "Education cannot be better described than by calling it the organization of acquired habits of conduct and tendencies to behavior.''—Talks to Teachers (New York, 1899), page 29.

Herbert Spencer: "To prepare us for complete living is the function which education has to discharge.''— Education (New York, 1872).

John Dewey: "I believe that education is the fundamental method of social progress and reform........I believe that education is a regulation of the process of coming to share in the social consciousness.''—My Pedagogic Creed (New York, 1897), page 16.

Arnold Tompkins: "The true end of teaching is one with the true aim of life; and each lesson must be presented with the conscious purpose of making the most out of the life of the one taught.''—The Philosophy of Teaching (Boston, 1895), page 71.

J. P. Munroe: "The question to be asked at the end of an educational step is not 'What has the child learned?' but 'What has the child become?' ''—The Educational Ideal (Boston, 1896), page 2.

inquirer to occupy the ethical standpoint.
Moreover, the ethical end is not thought of as
a far-off culmination of one's education, but
as an idea that is to be realized in every step
of the educational process. The child is to
grow continuously in the moral, as in the intellectual life, and these two aspects of life
are regarded as being properly inseparable.
Every study is to contribute directly to the
growth of the moral self. The school, in fact,
now becomes a miniature society united by
the ethical bond of regard for one another,
and each task is wrought with an ethical purpose or inspiration as real as that of mature
men in their respective callings.[1]

9. Education must take Cognizance of the true Nature and Destiny of Man. We are now in position to
formulate a general concep-
tion of education. Educa-
tion is any effort to assist
the development of an immature human being
toward the proper goal of life. This definition takes full account of the three factors
which we noted at the outset. It recognises the

[1] "I believe that the school is primarily a social institution. Education being a social process, the school
is simply the form of community life in which all those
agencies are concentrated that will be most effective in
bringing the child to share in the inherited resources of
the race, and to use his own powers for social ends. I
believe that education, therefore, is a process of living
and not a preparation for future living."—John Dewey:
My Pedagogic Creed (New York, 1897), page 7.

educator who makes the effort from the standpoint of maturity, the child with his laws of
development, and the truth that some kind of
life is better than other kinds. Yet the definition remains formal because it does not tell
us what sort of life is worth living and developing toward. It assumes the ethical point
of view, but it leaves the ethical ideal in un-
certainty. We make progress if we say that
the proper goal of life is social existence, and
so change our definition to the following:
Education is any effort to assist the development of an immature human being toward
social adjustment and efficiency. But we cannot rest in this definition unless we are will-
ing to say that the proper goal of life is
simply social adjustment and efficiency, and
nothing more. Certainly education cannot
accept as its end anything less than the highest destiny that man is capable of. Therefore,
any satisfactory answer to the question,
"What is education?" must include an answer to the question, "What is the highest
capacity of man?"

CHAPTER II

THE NECESSITY FOR RELIGIOUS EDUCATION

10. Religious Education is that which Recognises Man's Divine Destiny. We have just seen that education necessarily refers to the goal of life, whatever that goal may be. "The true end of teaching is one with the true aim of life." According to our conception of the meaning of life, then, will be our conception of education. He who regards the acquisition of mere things as man's supreme interest will think of education in narrowly utilitarian terms. To him it will signify apprenticeship to a trade, the mastery of manual and mental tools, the learning of such facts and the cultivation of such habits as will enable one to utilise nature's resources and get the better of one's fellows. On the other hand, he who thinks of life in ethical terms will think of education in ethical terms also. To him "the most truly practical education is that which imparts the most numerous and the strongest motives to noble action."[1] He realises that "none of us liveth to himself, and none dieth to himself," but

[1] Thomas Davidson : History of Education (New York, 1901), page 260.

rather that the individual can realise himself
only through society. Education then becomes a means of introducing young life to its
proper place in the social organism. If,
finally, we believe that complete self-realisation requires not only human society, but also
fellowship with God, then it follows that for
us education is the effort to assist immature
human beings toward complete self-realisation
in and through fellowship with both their fellows and God. Under this conception true
education does not stop with the development
of individual power, as under the first of the
notions just described, or with mere social
adjustment, as under the second, but it includes them both and also something more. It
aims at individual power, but forbids the
selfish use thereof; it aims at social adjustment, but holds that complete society includes
God and man.

11. It Aims (1) to Develop the Religious Nature. This standpoint may be
approached in three other
ways, from each of which
it receives further illumination. First, since
education is effort to develop the child, to
bring his germinal powers to maturity, we
may ask whether the child has a religious
nature, as he has also a social nature. The

detailed answer to this question, and the evidence therefor, will be given later. Here it is sufficient to note that the possession of a religious nature on the part of the child is a necessary presupposition of religious education. For, as we have already seen, to educate is not to secure conformity to adult ideas and practices, but to help the immature powers of the child to unfold and to grow. The demand for religious education that is being heard at the present day does not add anything to the formal conception of education as development of native capacities toward complete living, but it asserts that, just as the social destiny is pre-formed in the mental structure, so also is the religious destiny, and that in any complete education the one as well as the other must be developed.[1]

12. (2) To Transmit the Religious Heritage of the Race. We have just approached religious education through a consideration of the child. We may also approach it through the conception of the adult who undertakes to help the child. For, included in the accumulated experience whereby men are fitted to help childhood is religion. Butler

[1] See addresses by George A. Coe and Edwin D. Starbuck in Proceedings of The Religious Education Association (Chicago, 1903), pages 44-59.

defines education as "a gradual adjustment to the spiritual possessions of the race."[1] Under the term "spiritual possessions" he includes the scientific inheritance, the literary inheritance, the æsthetic inheritance, the institutional (or politico-social) inheritance, and the religious inheritance, to all five of which the child is entitled. Through long labor and pain, through experiment and reflection, the race has acquired ideas, habits, institutions, all of which are of recognised worth, but few of which could be acquired by anyone through his unaided powers even in the longest lifetime. Education puts each new generation into possession of these race-acquisitions. As someone has said, this enables each generation to stand upon the shoulders of the last. Applying this to religious education, we may say that it is the process whereby adults who have achieved something of right relations to their fellows and to God assist the young to reach similar relations.

13. (3) To Adjust the Race to its Divine Environment. The third method of approach borrows a biological notion. Life includes adjustment to environment, and the highest life is that which has the most

[1] Nicholas Murray Butler: The Meaning of Education (New York, 1898), Lecture I.

far-reaching adaptations. An animal with
eyes adjusts itself to distant objects, as well
as to those that are in contact with the body.
When memory appears it results in adaptation to the invisible and the future.
Mind as a whole can, in fact, be looked
upon as an instrument of adjustment.
Conscience and the social instinct bring
about conduct adapted to the social environment, and, if religion be true, the religious impulse adjusts the individual to God,
who environs us all. Under this biological
figure, education may be looked upon as a
special factor in the universal process of re-
lating living beings to their world, and religious education as the most universal or far-
reaching part thereof. Moreover, since the
religious aim in education includes the ethical
or social, religious education is the adaptation
not merely of individuals but also of society
or the species to the divine environment. Ac-
cepting the notion that education consists of
acts performed by society for social ends, we
reach this final outcome of our biological figure: In religious education organised man
provides for a progressive adaptation of the
race to its divine environment.[1]

[1] "Education is the eternal process of superior adjustment of the physically and mentally developed, free, con-

14. Religious Education not Distinguished by its Method. From every point of view, then, religious education is simply education that completes itself by taking account of the whole child, the whole educator, and the whole goal or destiny of man. It is not distinguished—primarily, at least, and in the sequel we shall see not at all—by any peculiarity of method or by any peculiarity in its means, such as the Bible, the catechism, or the personal influence of the parent or teacher. While it is inevitable that the details of material and of method will vary with varying conceptions of the end in view, the end, not the means, is the fundamental point of difference. The Sunday school is a *school* in the same sense as the public institution that bears that name. Home training is *training* in the same sense that the word "training" bears in either the Sunday school or the day school. Schools and training, of whatever kind, rest finally upon general laws of the mind and body of the being that is to be developed.

Perhaps the simplest illustration of this

scious, human being to God, as manifested in the intellectual, emotional, and volitional environment of man." —H. H. Horne: The Philosophy of Education (New York, 1904), page 285.

point is the law of habit. This law is basic in
all training whatsoever because it is the general method by which a movable element of
mind or character becomes a fixture. It applies to the intellect no more than it does to
the emotions; to the outward act no more than
to the inward motive or ideal. The only way
in which we can make what we wish to out
of an undeveloped being is to cause him to
form an appropriate habit. What is true of
the law of habit is true also of all the general
laws of the mind that underlie education.
They underlie all education, and necessarily
so. The primary difference between religious
and other education, accordingly, is the end
in view, or the conception of human life that
it represents.

**15. What is
"General"
Education?**
If, then, there is here any
fundamental antithesis at
all, it is not only an an-
tithesis; it is a conflict. For the sake of con-
venience of language, and especially because
the public schools of our country do not give
religious instruction, "general" education
has come to be distinguished not only from
technical and professional training but also
from training in religion. There results an
unfortunate habit of thought. Education in

religion is looked upon as a kind of special
training, or as a side current apart from the
main gulf-stream of culture. Like the training of bookkeepers, the study of Sanskrit, or
the exploration of the polar regions, it is supposed to pertain simply to those who have a
special interest therein. The Sunday school,
and even religious training within the family
are therefore regarded as mere appendages of
the educational system. But religious education can no more accept this place than religion itself can consent to be a mere department of life. If religion were just a specialty
of priests, monks, and nuns; or if it belonged
to Sunday, but not to week days; or if it applied to only a part of our conduct and our
ideals, then, indeed, religious education and
general education might be contrasted with
each other. In that case we would do well to
change our terminology. Reserving the term
education to designate the development of the
man as such, we should use the term training
to indicate the special preparation for a particular occupation or function, as medical,
legal, business, or religious training. But religion claims to belong to the man as such. It
assumes to include morals, or the relations
between man and man, and indeed to reach to

every aim or ideal whatsoever. Whatever religion may have been to early man, and whatever it may be to other civilisations than our
own, to us it is an all-inclusive, all-command-
ing principle, the very stuff that human life
is made of, or it is nothing at all. Consequently, for us religious education is simply
education in the complete sense of that term,
or else it is not education, but mere special
training. It is therefore not strictly correct
to call it a part, even a necessary part, of
general education. Special times and places
and material may, of course, be set apart with
a special view to the religious development of
the child, but only in order that his whole
development, in every department, may be
raised to the religious level.[1]

16. The Unity of Education: (1) From the Psychological Point of View.   In reality we have here
reached the principle of the
unity of education. The
principle asserts that education is not made up by aggregating

[1] Nicholas Murray Butler opposes the use of the
term 'religious education' on the ground that education
is a unitary process and that religious training, intellectual training, etc., apart from the whole, have no real
existence as education.—See Lecture I in Principles of
Religious Education (New York, 1900). With this general point of view I think we may agree at the same
time that we employ the term religious education to
designate—not a part of general education, but—the
essential character of any truly general development of
the human person.

parts, each of which exists on its own account, but that it is rather like the single life that realises itself in the various organs of a human body. The reasons for this point of view are three-fold. In the first place, the child himself is a unit. He is not a bundle of faculties—an intellect, *plus* a will, *plus* a heart, etc. The old fashioned faculty-psychology, which thus divided the man, is a thing of the past. The whole child is at work in each of his studies, not memory in one, reason in another, perception in a third; and if the teacher cannot get the whole child thus engaged the effort at teaching fails. The idea of education, accordingly, is not that the child acquires first one thing, then another, but that he *is* first one thing, and then he develops into something different. The principle of unity thus carries us back once more to the ethical conception of education, that is, the conception of what the child is becoming.

17. (2) From the Ethical Point of View. From the ethical point of view, also, we quickly discover that education, rightly considered, is a unit. For the ethical view of life is an effort to introduce into life, or to discover within life, organisation, harmony, unity. We begin our existence as creatures of mere impulse. The little child is absorbed first in one situation, then in another; he does not connect them or feel the need of doing so; as far as his consciousness goes, life is framentary and unorganised. What education has to do for him is to bring into his impulses due subordination of one to another; into his fragmentary interests a principle of organisation; into his life as a whole a purpose and a meaning. That is, he is to develop toward an ideal self, and this ideal presides as mistress over the whole process. Education is unitary, then, not merely because in the actual self of the child there is no separation of faculties, but also because the ideal of a completely unified self is an implicit principle of the whole development.

18. (3) From the Religious Point of View. The unified self with which ethics has to do is, of course, the social self, or the self realised in society. Religion alone, in strictness, looks to that complete unification of the self which includes not only my fellows but also my entire world. Ethics as such is usually considered as having to do merely with human relationships; religion with our relations to the ultimate ground of our being. Now, whether or not religious faith is well founded, the aspiration for unity with the ultimate ground of our being is implicit in all education. The endeavor of all of us as men is to find ourselves at home in this our world. The practical interest in controlling nature and the theoretical interest in knowing her blend into the one interest of overcoming the apparent opposition between the self and its world. Self-realisation can never be complete except as an ultimate unity is found here. Thus religion, instead of being a department of education, is an implicit motive thereof. It is the end that presides over the beginning and gives unity to all stages of the process.

CHAPTER III

GOD, NATURE, AND MAN IN EDUCATION

19. The Narrow and the Broad Sense of "Education." Thus far we have considered education simply as a voluntary activity on the part of men, an effort of the older to help the younger. This is education in the narrow or strictly technical sense. But there is a larger sense of the term, also, according to which it designates everything that enters into the process of shaping the character of the child, and finally everything that shapes mankind in the large.[1] Thus we speak of the education of a nation, as Israel, or of the human race, as well as of individuals. We say, also, that nature helps in various ways to educate the race and the individual, and that "experience is a stern school-master." In the present chapter an effort will be made to view religious education in this large way, and especially to connect the two obvious factors in it, man the educator

[1] Cf. J. K. F. Rosenkranz: The Philosophy of Education (New York, 1889), pages 10, 21f.

and nature the educator, with God as educator in the supreme sense.

20. The Divine Education of Israel. The thought that God educates men is a very old one. "The law," says the Letter to the Galatians (3: 24) "hath been our tutor to bring us unto Christ." This appears to have been the general standpoint of the early Christians with reference to the history of Israel. That history was a divine preparation of the nation for receiving the supreme revelation in Christ. God spoke to the fathers through the prophets, and by this means gradually brought about the fulness of the time that made the sending of his own Son a practicable measure. Herein the early Christians did not read the notion of race education into the ancient scriptures; it was already there, and very close to the surface, too. The story of Israel is a story of growth from small beginnings to a great nation; of the setting of tasks, of specific instruction, of testing, punishing and rewarding, all with a view to bringing to maturity the "son" who was "called out of Egypt" (Hosea, 11: 1). Jehovah was a father, and Israel was a child who was being brought up.

21. The Divine Education of the Race. By extending this notion just a little farther, we come to think of divine providence in the whole of human history as a divine education of the race. God does not merely judge the nations, punishing evil and rewarding good; he also trains the nations toward righteousness. The growth of civilisation is the progress of mankind in this divine school. Particularly in the history of religion do we find this manifest. Lessing, and the philosophers of religion who have built upon his great conception of the divine education of the human race, have taught us to see in the religions of the world a gradual self-revelation of God to men. This is a modern idea, and yet the roots of it were certainly present in the mind of Paul when he proclaimed his philosophy of religion to the Athenians. God, he declared, not only created men, but also appointed their national existence, and implanted in them an impulse to seek after him. Further, God recognises, as flowing from this divinely implanted impulse, lower as well as higher stages of religion, and in Christ he brings to a culmination what was dimly revealed even in ignorant modes of worship (Acts 17: 22-30). At a later point in our study we shall see how true it is that the race begins its career in an infantile state and moves toward maturity only through a gradual process of education.

22. The Divine Education of the Individual. But the race consists of individuals, and so the divine education of the race is the divine education of individual boys and girls. Boys and girls, let us say, rather than men and women. For the plasticity that is pre-requisite to education largely disappears when youth passes into full manhood and womanhood. Maturity is, indeed, the great period for acquiring things and knowledge, but not for forming character. As far as race progress in character is concerned, the chief contribution that maturity can make is to accumulate the means and instruments for making the next generation better than the present through improved education.[1] If God is

---

[1] "I believe that education is the fundamental method of social progress and reform......I believe that all reforms which rest simply upon the enactment of law, or the threatening of certain penalties, or upon changes in mechanical or outward arrangements, are transitory and futile....I believe that the community's duty to education is, therefore, its paramount moral duty. By law and punishment, by social agitation and discussion, society can regulate and form itself in a more or less haphazard and chance way. But through education society can formulate its own purposes, can organise its own means and resources, and thus shape itself with definiteness in the direction in which it wishes to move."—John Dewey: My Pedagogic Creed (New York, 1897), pages 16 f.

the supreme educator of the race, he is for
the same reason the supreme educator of each
child. This aspect of the educational problem has been almost entirely overlooked, even
by religious teachers. Education has been
persistently thought of as something done for
the child by his elders, while the possibility
that it may consist still more in something
wrought within the character by the Divine
Spirit has been scarcely dreamed of. It will
therefore be worth while to see how we are to
connect the thought of God as the great educator of the race with the humble, everyday
effort of parent or teacher to bring up a child
in the way that he should go.

**23. The Divine
Hand in the
Religious Nature
of Man.**
First of all, the child
comes forth from God bearing the image of the Crea-
tor. That God created man
in his own image may once have seemed to
imply many grotesque notions of God, as that
he has a physical form which ours resembles.
But the phrase never loses its power over us
because, with every advance in our conceptions of God, we discover something corresponding thereto in the structure of our own
mind. Man has a religious nature. The definite establishment of this proposition is per-

haps the greatest service that the history and psychology of religion have performed. Not very long ago men were still asking whether religion might not have arisen through priest-craft or statecraft, or at least through some incidental feature of human experience. Religion was looked upon as a theory or belief which men had formed for themselves somewhat as we form our hypotheses of inhabitants in other planets. Some tribes were said to be entirely without religion, and hence it was inferred that religion does not belong to humanity as such. But the 'tribe destitute of religion' is found to be purely imaginary, and the history of religion begins its recital with the affirmation that man as such has a religious impulse out of which have sprung all the religions of the world.[1]

Out of this impulse springs, not less, the entire religious development of the individual. Here is something that neither parent nor teacher imparts, something that must first be there if their labor is to have any religious effectiveness. Into the constitution of every one of us God has wrought his plan for human life. In every genuine utterance of the religious impulse

[1] See, for example, Morris Jastrow: The Study of Religion (New York, 1901), pages 195 f., 293, *et passim.*

there is manifested 'prevenient grace,' the
divine empowering and inspiration that
'come before' our human acts and give them
effect.   Thus, at every step in religious education God himself—the present, living God,
the Word that enlighteneth every man coming
into the world—is the supreme factor.

24. The Divine Vocation of Parents and Teachers.   It follows that parents
and teachers are properly
instruments in the divine
hand for playing upon the
divinely constructed strings of human nature.
Man as educator is not the complete source of
his own activities.   His desire to build up
right character in the young is not an invention, it is an inspiration.   The same hand that
impels the child through what we call the
religious impulse impels the educator also to
supply food for the growth of that impulse.
And what a vocation is this of parents and
teachers!   In their hands as in no others lie
the reins of the chariot of God.   In the nature of things, the kingdom of God must
grow chiefly by securing control of young
life.   The religious impulse must be fed and
it must be led on to realise its full manhood
through voluntary obedience to Christ.   This
is religious education.   It controls the stream

at its source. The broad river of humanity is
what it is made to be in the home and in the
school of whatever kind. Parents and teachers are making history; they are making or
unmaking civilisation; they are promoting or
holding back the triumph of God's kingdom
upon the earth. They are doing this whether
they will or no. The young life that touches
their life is plastic. It takes the shape of that
with which it comes into contact. Every parent, every teacher, and indeed every person
who has any relation to young life has therefore a divine vocation. He is set apart,
chosen, to reveal God. This is true of irreligious as well as religious parents, of teachers in the week-day school as well as teachers
in the Sunday school. Whoever is placed where
he molds the life of a child or youth, however
he came to be so placed, is bound to this service.

25. Nature as a Factor in Education. The educational reform
of the last century is char-
acterised chiefly by two
marks: On the one hand, it gives a new recognition to natural law in the educational
process, and on the other hand it defines the
end of education in social terms. The nature-
side appears most prominently in the extraor-

dinary attention given to the child—his physical and mental structure, his spontaneous
impulses, the stages of his growth, and the
relation of his development to the evolution
of the human species. We have come to see
that education is not imposed by us upon nature but is rather a voluntary carrying forward of a natural process. Every sensation
that streams in upon the infant mind contributes something to the formation of the personality. The baby's spontaneous throwing
about of arms and legs helps to develop the
motor centers which constitute the physical
basis of will and self-control. Play is a genuine school in which nature drills the pupil
in every faculty. The whole contact of the
child with nature is, in fact, educative. But
even this is not half the story. For in the
spontaneous reactions which the child makes
to his environment we behold adaptive mental
traits which he has inherited through
his relation to the species, and the species
through its place in the general evolution of
living beings. The past of the race speaks in
the child, and the past of life upon this
planet speaks in the race. The social instinct,
for example, which is one of the corner stones
of all character-building, is natural in the

complete sense of the term nature, and it has
a long human and pre-human history. All
our deliberate efforts to educate can do no
more than continue the work thus begun by
nature. We do not bestow a mental constitution upon the child; we merely feed, stimulate, and direct what is already there. We
may say, therefore, that education carries forward what nature has already begun.[1]

**26. The Educative
Presence of God
in Nature.**
What then? Shall we
think that, because education is natural, God is not a
factor in it? Rather, let us say that, just because evolution has provided a basis upon
which our spiritual building can be erected,
just because the movement of life has been
upward toward the capacity and the impulse
of love toward God, therefore we discover God

[1] "Education is conscious or voluntary evolution."—
Thomas Davidson: History of Education (New York,
1901), page 1. Cf. Nicholas Murray Butler: The
Meaning of Education (New York, 1898), Lecture I,
and the following words from Bishop Spalding: "Life
is the unfolding of a mysterious power, which in man
rises to self-consciousness, and through self-consciousness to the knowledge of a world of truth and order
and love, where action may no longer be left wholly
to the sway of matter or to the impulse of instinct,
but may and should be controlled by reason and conscience. To further this process by deliberate and intelligent effort is to educate. Hence education is man's
conscious co-operation with the Infinite Being in promoting the development of life; it is the bringing of
life in its highest form to bear upon life, individual and
social, that it may raise it to greater perfection, to ever-
increasing potency."—J. L. Spalding: Means and Ends
of Education (Chicago, 1901), page 72.

in evolution and conclude that the ultimate source of education as respects nature, the child, and the educator—all three—is He in whom "we live, and move, and have our being."[1] This way of regarding nature is completed in the universally received doctrine of the immanence, or abiding presence, of God. This means, among other things, that material atoms are forms of divine activity; that the laws of nature are simply the orderly methods of his rational will, which is in complete control of itself; that evolution does not suffer any break when man, a self conscious and moral being, appears, because the whole of evolution is, in reality, a process of realising a moral purpose; that the correlation of mind and brain is just the phenomenal aspect of the real correlation of our mind with the divine power which sustains us; that the development, physiological and mental, that man receives through nature is part of an all-inclusive educational plan, and that, in our work as educators, God is working through our reason and will to carry forward the universal plan.

---

[1] See Newman Smyth: Through Science to Faith (New York, 1902) ; also Henry Drummond: The Ascent of Man (New York, 1898).

CHAPTER IV

THE CHRISTIAN VIEW OF CHILDHOOD

27. Jesus and Little Children. The inclusion of nature and the spiritual life of man in a single conception, as was done in the last chapter, brings us face to face with the Christian conceptions of the natural and the spiritual man, of depravity and grace, as far as these have a bearing upon childhood. We must, in short, go forward from the standpoint of religious education in a merely general sense to that of specifically Christian education.

The central idea, the controlling principle of such education, must be sought in the life and teachings of Jesus. Here we are at once struck by a distinctive attitude and a distinctive utterance. It is clear that Jesus was fond of children; he had the same tender feeling, the same *belief* in them that every normal man among us experiences who comes close to the life of a little one. To Jesus child-life is not a dark picture, but a bright one. It does not depress his soul with a sense of evil or of danger, but lifts it up with a feeling of the nearness of divine things. We should find this in the picture of Jesus taking little chil-

dren into his arms, even if he had left no recorded word on the subject. But he expressly
declares this to be his view. He took little
children into his arms and "blessed them."
The word here rendered "blessed" has the
same root as our term "eulogy," and in this
particular passage the simple root is strength-
ened by a special prefix that denotes intensity.
The root-meaning, "to speak well of," has acquired various derivative meanings, but it is
a word that could not be used of a person or a
thing that one did not approve of.

**28. Jesus' Teach-
ing Concerning
the Child and the
Kingdom.** This of itself would be
enough to let us know the
mind of the Master concerning childhood. But the
Master put his thought into still more specific
form. "For of such," he said, "is the kingdom of God." The "of such" is a possessive;
it is the same form as the "theirs" in the first
Beatitude, "Blessed are the poor in spirit,
for theirs is the kingdom of heaven." That is,
Jesus asserts that the kingdom of God belongs to little children, it is theirs. The statement is not that the kingdom belongs to those
who are *like* little children—that is a separate statement which refers to adults.
Adults who are at enmity with God must enter

the kingdom by humbling themselves and becoming like little children, but to little children themselves the kingdom already belongs. It may, perhaps, be significant that
this passage occurs in the oldest of the Gos-
pels, that of Mark. Additional weight is
given to it by Jesus' repeated references to
childhood as an illustration of the qualities
necessary for entering the kingdom and for
attaining greatness therein.

29. Jesus' View of the Child's Spiritual Development. A distinction is made, then, between the status of little children and that of mature and wilful sinners. The latter must repent and be converted, but children, already possessing the life-principle of the kingdom, require spiritual development. Jesus' recorded words do not, it is true, say all this, yet all of it is implied in the circum-stances under which he spoke the words that have come down to us. He was speaking to a Jewish audience. Now, as soon as we realise the sense that a Jewish hearer must have found in his words, they become illuminated for us. Every Jewish child, by virtue of his blood, was regarded as under the covenant made with Abraham; he was already a mem-ber of the theocratic kingdom. In no sense was he an outsider who had to be brought in. According to the law he was simply to be taught from infancy the story of Israel, a story in which he belonged from birth, and when he reached the age of thirteen he became, as a matter of course, subject to the whole law. This conception of childhood Jesus here adopts, spiritualises, and fills with his own good news of the kingdom, not of Israel, but of God. As the Jewish child was within the Abrahamic covenant by virtue of descent from Abraham, so all children are within the household of God by virtue of the divine grace which Jesus here announces. Normal child development, then, takes place entirely within the kingdom of grace. It consists of a gradual apprehension of the principles of the kingdom, and increasing participation in the activities and responsibilities thereof. The parables of the growth of the kingdom apply to the individual as well as to the world at large. In both spheres the law is "first the blade, then the ear, then the full corn in the ear."

30. What should Christians Expect of their Children?   We shall see, after a while, that the assumption of responsibility by the Jewish child at the age of thirteen is a normal and typical fact. A transition more or less rapid, more or less profound, is to be looked for in the early and middle years of adolescence. But children should be expected to remain within the kingdom from infancy, so that the adolescent transition, when it comes, may be a step, not into the Christian life, but within the Christian life. Many children of Christian parents do, as a matter of fact, reach Christian manhood in this way. Taught from the start to count themselves children of God, from stage to stage of their growth they exercise a faith that is proportioned to their powers. These represent the normal development of a child under Christian influences. The fact that many children who are brought up in Christian homes go away from God does not indicate that Jesus was in error in his view of the child and his development. He knew that tares may spring up in any wheat field, and that in the child as well as in the adult the kingdom wages a contest with evil. But who shall say how much of this falling away is due to a general failure on the part of the church to apprehend Jesus' plan of the kingdom? Many Christian parents assume that their children are aliens or outsiders who must wait to scription of the torments of literal hell fire.

In song, if anywhere, the heart of Jesus should find expression, yet in a collection of "Hymns for Sunday Schools, Youth and Children"[1] published as late as 1852, the child is made to sing from the standpoint of human ruin and fear. Compare the following child's hymn, for example, with the words of Jesus concerning childhood:

> "There is beyond the sky
>   A heaven of joy and love ;
> And holy children, when they die,
>   Go to that world above.
>
> "There is a dreadful hell,
>   And everlasting pains ;
> There sinners must with devils dwell,
>   In darkness, fire, and chains.
>
> "Can such a child as I
>   Escape this awful end?
> And may I hope, whene'er I die,
>   I shall to heaven ascend?
>
> "Then will I read and pray,
>   While I have life and breath ;
> Lest I should be cut off to-day,
>   And sent t' eternal death."

33. The Doctrinal Difficulty has been Overcome. The difficulty for education that grows out of the doctrine of depravity is practically overcome in some churches through the countervailing doctrine of baptismal regeneration. This provides for spiritual life in all baptised infants and makes genuine Chris-

---

[1] New York, Carlton & Phillips, 1852. I have made further citations from this interesting collection in The Religion of a Mature Mind (Chicago, 1902), pages 314 f.

tian nurture possible. In other churches the
difficulty had to be met by a new adjustment
of the notions of sin and grace, and this adjustment has actually been made. We owe it,
in large measure, to Horace Bushnell who,
just before the publication of the hymn just
quoted, issued his book on Christian Nurture
(1847). He maintained that a positive religious life does not need to wait for the crisis
of conversion, but that, under the pervasive
influence of the Christian family, ''the child
should grow up a Christian, and never know
himself as being otherwise.'' To the objec-
tion that this theory ignores the child's depravity and the necessity for regeneration,
Bushnell replied in substance that wherever
sin can abound there grace can much more
abound. That is, he overcame the difficulty,
not by denying depravity, but by exalting
the grace of God. The unquestionably good
qualties shown by little children he interpreted as signs of the divine in-working.
With this in-working parents and teachers
are to co-operate so that development of the
divinely implanted germ may be continuous.

A similar position was taken a little later
by F. G. Hibbard, who approached the problem from Arminian rather than Puritan pre-

suppositions.[1] He maintained that children —all children—are in a state of favor with God, who imparts to them a genuine spiritual quickening or principle of life. This view he supports at length from Scripture and from the current belief of his own communion that all chidren who die in infancy are saved. If dying infants are saved, it must be through divine grace, but why should such grace be given to those who die, but withheld from those who need it for living? This view requires a change in the ordinary notion of conversion, for now the real question becomes—not, Will this child ever be converted to God? but—Will he ever be converted away from God? One cannot become a member of the kingdom of sin except through one's own evil choice to surrender one's heavenly citizenship.

Through such writings and other influences there has come to prevail somewhat generally the view that the Holy Spirit is continually present in the heart of man from the beginning of consciousness, and that thus a genuine spiritual life is imparted, in germinal form, to

[1] F. G. Hibbard: The Religion of Childhood; or, Children in their Relation to Native Depravity, to the Atonement, to the Family, and to the Church (Cincinnati: Poe & Hitchcock, 1866).

all who do not positively refuse to accept it. The existence of evil tendencies is not thereby denied, but such tendencies are believed to find a continuous corrective in divine help as far as this is not rejected or neglected. Neither is the need of individual decision lessened under this view, for normal growth takes place only through co-operation of the individual will with the inner divine impulsion.

34. Good and Evil Impulses in Children. This change in the doctrinal point of view has been accompanied by more thorough observation of the actual impulses of children. The general result thereof is to confirm the universal Christian belief that, in some sense, the natural man is at enmity with the spiritual man. At the same time it shows that the natural man is, in some sense, already spiritual. The impulses of children are partly wholesome, partly unwholesome.

It is clear that children's "lies," which were formerly regarded as clear evidence of childhood depravity, have been misunderstood. In order to recognise the difference between fact and fancy, considerable experience is necessary. Even grown persons commonly confuse the two. How much more a little child, who has everything yet to

learn! Moreover, even when this distinction is realised, the child may not understand the moral quality of wilful deception. He deceives in self-defense just as he raises his arm to ward off a blow. He has still to learn the social effect of a lie. In short, when we look at children's falsehoods from the standpoint of the child himself we discover no such inbred evil as was once assumed to be there.

Similarly the cruelty that is attributed to little children is probably not cruelty at all. For the young child has had no experience that enables him to interpret the signs of suffering in animals or in men. He does not delight in inflicting pain upon others, for he does not realise that he is inflicting pain. He has, however, great curiosity to see what will happen, and he delights to feel his own power through witnessing the effects of it in the reactions of living things. At these points, then, childhood's impulses are not as bad as they have been represented to be.

At certain other points, however, the young child displays impulses that are little above those of the brutes. Every infant, to begin with, is an almost complete egoist. His greed is boundless; he is subject to unregulated an-

ger and envy; he resists all the restraints that are essential to social existence. On the other hand, germs of positive good, such as sympathy, kindness, generosity, affection, spring up very early and in advance of instruction and moral reflection.[1]

35. How Interpret these Impulses? Thus good and evil impulses mix in every child. Yet not "good and evil" in any complete sense. We must, in fact, make still another effort to see the facts from the point of view of childhood itself. Greed and anger that would be reprehensible in us may bear no such character in an infant. "No such *character*"; that is precisely it. Character is a confirmed habit of moral choice, and this the young child has not yet attained. It would be well, therefore, to drop both adjectives, "evil" and "good," in our description of childhood, at least of young childhood, or else learn to give them an unwonted meaning. The child has not a character as yet; he is merely a candidate for character. He *is* neither good nor bad; he is merely *becoming* one or the other. Some of his impulses, if they grow unchecked and unregulated, will

[1] On this whole subject, see James Sully: Studies of Childhood (New York, 1900), Chapter VII.

issue in bad character; others, if they grow
symmetrically, will result in good character.
That is the whole story.

No, not quite the whole. For the two sets
of impulses do not stand on quite the same
footing. One set relates the child to the
lower animals, the other to distinctly human
life. The law of evolution has for the first
time enabled us to see such facts in their true
perspective. The unlovely impulses are traces
of lower orders of life out of which man has
evolved, and out of which each individual
child develops. The individual begins life on
the animal plane, somewhat as the human
race did, and he has to attain through development the distinctly human traits. But *it
is natural that he should attain them.*[1] The
law of development is written in his members.
The lower tendencies are, indeed, natural in
the sense that they spontaneously appear and
actually compete with the higher; but in a
profounder sense of "natural" the higher
tendencies are the natural ones, in the sense,
namely, that they represent what both the

[1] Comenius, one of the earliest founders of natural
method, says: "It is more natural and, through the
grace of the Holy Spirit, easier for a man to become
wise, honest, and righteous, than for his progress to be
hindered by incidental depravity."—John Amos Comenius :
The Great Didactic, Translated by W. M. Keatinge (London, 1896), p. 203.

child and the race are becoming. In order
to live his own life the child must control
and regulate his impulses. He not only
must but also does discriminate between
them, and generally he identifies himself
with at least a part of the general group
of impulses that we call wholesome. Finally, as will be shown in the proper place,
even the impulses that we call lower are capable of being transformed into instruments
for the realisation of the higher nature.
Greed, anger, envy, all represent spontaneous
energy that can be directed into either useful
or harmful channels. The work of education,
accordingly, is to furnish nutriment for the
higher tendencies and direction for the lower.

36. A Positive Religious Nature is Presupposed in Religious Education. We are now ready to see
how these facts bear upon
religious education. First,
the denial of a positive re-
ligious nature to man through the doctrine of
total depravity tended to paralyse religious
education. (*a*) It denied that there was anything to develop. (*b*) It judged the child
from the standpoint of the adult, and therefore could not secure any natural leverage in
the child-mind. (*c*) It employed repression,
instead of securing expression, with the

result of distorting the personality, and often of producing opposition to religion. (*d*) Taking maturity as a standard, it encouraged religious precocity, which is clearly unwholesome. (*e*) It placed undue emphasis upon conversion experiences, and this led, on the one hand, to emotional excesses, and on the other to unnatural (and unspiritual) straining after subjective states.

Education in religion must start out, then, with the assumption that the child has a positive religious nature. This does not imply any of the following notions: (*a*) That the child is 'all right' as he is. Even a mature Christian is not 'all right.' Both must struggle to maintain and to increase the life that is within them, and both may stumble without forfeiting that life. (*b*) That the child can grow up properly by a merely 'natural' process, without divine help. Even a mature Christian needs daily help. (*c*) That the life principle in the child can take care of itself without our help. On the contrary, just because a positive religious nature is here, definite spiritual food must be supplied. (*d*) That the child has any definitely conscious religious experience or sense of God. He is merely *becoming conscious of spiritual* things.

To speak positively, the possession of a positive religious nature implies three things: (a) That the child has more than a passive capacity for spiritual things. Just as animals go forth in search of food, so a positive spiritual nature goes forth spontaneously in search of God. (b) That nothing short of union with God can really bring a human being to himself. The absurdity of a miser's life is that a heart that hungers for God feeds on gold. The tragedy in the life of every voluptuary is that a few drops of pleasure are offered to slake a thirst for eternal things. In fact, in all our strivings for wealth, pleasure, honor, culture, we are really seeking to satisfy a divine craving. The real meaning of everything with which we have to do is God, who is in all and through all. Failing to find him, we lose even our self. (c) That the successive phases in the growth of the child personality may be, and normally are, so many phases of a growing consciousness of the divine meaning of life. Both the idea of God and the religious regulation of life can develop from crude beginnings, just as the song of a lark comes out of a songless egg. In Part II we shall have to show how the religious demand

of the child utters itself, and how the religious nature grows.

37. Resulting Conception of Christian Education. We saw in the last chapter how it is possible to include God, nature, and man in a unitary conception of religious education. At last, after a long discussion, we are ready to include Christ in the same conception, and thus rise to the thought of distinctively Christian education. The view of God in his world that was suggested in the last chapter is the Christian view. The Christian view of the child fits therein perfectly. In the spontaneous life of the young child, all free from calculation and deliberate choice, we see the human life of love and reverence emerging out of nature. Here the meaning of nature begins to show itself; here creation rises from its valleys and plains toward the mountain summits. God himself makes the heart hungry. But where shall nutriment adequate to this creature's demands be found? Here is appetite of a new and surprising sort. What is man? He has been made only a little lower than God. He has been crowned with glory and honor, and all things have been put under his feet. Yet even that is not enough for him. He will

have conscious union with the one being who is higher than himself. Now, Christianity says that in Christ God gives himself to men as their light, their bread, their life. Children, all of us, apprehending reality first of all through sensuous media, we receive God through his historic manifestation in that which we can see with our eyes, and that which we can handle with our hands of the Word of Life. In Christ God responds to our hunger. Feeding upon him we grow in likeness to God; that is, we develop, we are educated. Christian education consists, then, in so presenting Christ to immature souls that they shall be by him enlightened, inspired, and fed according to their gradually increasing capacity, and thus made to grow continuously within the courts of the Lord's house.

APPENDIX TO CHAPTER IV

EDUCATION, DEPRAVITY, AND THE BIRTH FROM ABOVE

I believe that one of the most serious obstacles to the proper training of children is to be found in the inertia of outgrown or misunderstood theological conceptions. One of the most misunderstood of these conceptions is that of the "new birth" as it is related to the normal development of the religious consciousness. Education and regeneration have been habitually contrasted with each other, as though Jesus, in his declaration to Nicodemus, had in mind suddenness or any other temporal conception rather than the qualitative unlikeness of two kinds of life and the divine source of one of them. It would be well to go back to the primary meaning of the scriptural words by speaking of the "birth from above" rather than the "new" birth. The life from above is a *kind* of life, and its source is God. There is here no antithesis to education or development. A mature Christian is expected to grow in the divine life; why may not a child grow in it also? Why may not the

life be there from the start? Education does
not bestow it upon the child, or enable him
to create it for himself; it merely helps him,
as the usual means of grace help adult Christians, to work out what God works within. A
child who thus grows up has the life from
above as truly as a converted rebel. Receiving as he goes along "the true light, even the
light that lighteth every man as he cometh
into the world," he has a right to be called a
child of God. (*Cf.* George A. Coe: The Religion of a Mature Mind (Chicago, 1902),
Chapter VII: "The Right to be Called a
Child of God").

That the present theological standpoint
of leading Christian denominations fur-
nishes, in nearly every case, an adequate
theoretical basis for Christian education is
reasonably clear from a survey of our present situation. The Presbyterian General
Assembly has declared that all children who
die in infancy are saved. Here it is proper to
apply the remark of Hibbard already referred
to (see page 54). *Cf.* Henry VanDyke: God
and Little Children (New York, 1890). A
well known Presbyterian clergyman, in response to a question, writes to me as follows:
"The Presbyterian doctrine concerning the

relation of young children to God is this:
That by original nature, in their first state,
they are in a state of deficiency, needing the
touch of divine grace with regenerative power
before they are made the subjects of salvation. . . This touch of divine grace or
regenerative presence in the child life may
come at birth, or, as I believe and I think
others do, may come before birth or quickly
after. It is a point, of course, upon which
there can be no knowledge, but the point is
that the child in its infant days becomes the
subject of regeneration, and is never really
alienated from God, but from birth is his
child and may and should grow up into a
simple, normal, filial relation.'' Accordingly,
''in the belief of our church young people are
born members of the church.''

A representative Congregationalist makes a
similar answer. After making allowance for
differences between congregations, he says:
''The general faith is that all young children
are, even though unconsciously, the children
of God, and in the normal development of the
child's soul its relation changes only as the
relation of the child changes to the external
world.''

The Methodist position, which is based upon

a tendency to magnify the free grace of God, is the same. The emphasis which the Wesleyan movement has always placed upon conversion has undoubtedly brought about a somewhat general expectation that even children who have enjoyed Christian training will pass through a crisis of repentance and conversion. Yet a long succession of the leading authorities of Wesleyanism, of whom Hibbard is an example, has taken the position that a child may grow to maturity entirely within the kingdom of God. John Wesley, Fletcher, Watson, Adam Clarke, Whedon, have all asserted it. See article on "Wesley and other Methodist Fathers on Childhood Religion," by C. W. Rishell in Methodist Review, September-October, 1902; also R. J. Cooke: Christianity and Childhood (New York, 1891), and article by J. A. Story on "The Religion of Childhood" in Methodist Review, July-August, 1900.

Of thirty-four candidates for the ministry of the English Wesleyan church who were recently called upon to relate their religious experience, considerably less than half, according to a report in the Methodist Recorder for August 6, 1903, mentioned any definite time or place of conversion, while many distinctly testified that their religious life had been a gradual growth from childhood.

A representative Baptist clergyman says on the same point: "It is the general belief that young children are God's children, and will be saved if they die in that early stage; that they inherit evil tendencies which are sure to manifest themselves as they develop, and these tendencies, consented to and intensified by the personal will, are so radical and strong that they call for what the Scripture designates "regeneration," a spiritual crisis wrought by the Spirit of God. This crisis may be according to age, temperament and previous moral conduct, sudden and marked or almost imperceptible, like the dawn of day. In a normal life there comes a time of decision, when the soul yields to God or pulls away; the latter act makes the accountable child a wayward child, a sinner condemned."

CHAPTER V

THE CHARACTERISTICS OF MODERN EDUCATION

38. Three Contrasts between Mediæval and Modern Education. The characteristics of modern education may be studied from either of two points of view. We may observe the school itself—the teaching force, the controlling bodies, the material of instruction, the relation of the curriculum to life—or we may note the movement of educational theory in the works of writers on this subject. In the present section the former method will be used. If we compare mediæval with modern schools, three contrasts will strike us at once. *First,* mediæval teachers were practically all clergymen or other church functionaries, while the teaching force of modern schools is drawn chiefly from the laity. *Second,* the control of mediæval schools was vested in the church, while that of modern schools is vested chiefly in the state. *Third,* the point of view of the school has changed from that of preparation for personal salvation through believing dogmas authoritatively handed down by the church to that of preparation for the common life, particularly the life of society, by the acquisition of so-called secular knowledge.

At first sight the contrast here seems to be very sharp. The mediæval school had in view the eternal salvation of the soul; the modern school, the living of our temporal life. The mediæval school was "scholastic," the modern is "scientific." Scholasticism means the carrying on of all studies, all intellectual work, under the assumption that beliefs formulated by the church have final authority, so that they may not be inquired into in the sense of being tested. On the other hand, the scientific spirit is that of free inquiry. It recognises no authority for the inquiring mind except that of fact and of reasoned truth. It assumes the right to test all things and hold fast only that which stands the test. Its chief concern is not to maintain what is already accepted as true, but rather to extend the bounds of certain knowledge. The function of discovering new knowledge pertains, of course, to no educational institution below the university, but the spirit of science permeates modern schools of all grades.[1]

[1] The term science is used in English in two or more senses. In the narrower sense it means the natural and physical sciences; in the broader sense it signifies all

39. Apparent Conflict between Modern Education and Religion. These three contrasts show what is meant by the statement that the modern school is "secular," while the mediæval school was religious. At first sight, the "secularisation" of the schools appears to involve a conflict with religion. For, while religion demands submission, the spirit of modern education encourages individual judgment. The church asserts that this or that is true, basing its assertion upon divine revelation; the spirit of the school authorises each man to inquire for himself whether it is true or not. Religion talks of unseen realities, while modern education turns attention more and more to things that can be seen and handled. Religion makes God the first and supreme interest, but the "secular" school avoids speaking of God, and leaves to outside or incidental agencies the chief, and possibly the only, development that the child's religious nature receives.

knowledge that is based upon the scientific method, *viz.*, observation and analysis. "The scientific spirit" has reference solely to the method of study, that is, the method which bases conclusions on observed facts and just reasonings therefrom rather than upon authority, speculation, argument, etc. This commonplace remark is made here because popular religious discussions frequently use the terms science and scientific as though they referred simply to the habitual points of view or characteristic methods of the physical and natural sciences.

It is therefore of the highest importance
to inquire how much of real conflict there
is here. Is the modern school either a rival
or an opponent of religion? In principle,
as we shall see, it is not, but in its
practical working at some times and in
some places it may and probably does hinder
religion. In fact, purely secular education
is a reaction from the one-sidedness of
the mediæval schools, and as a reaction it
is itself one-sided. There may be adequate
reason why state schools should abstain from
positive religious instruction, but in that case
state schools cannot be regarded as more than
a part of a proper educational system. Religious education there must be, either within
or without the state schools. If modern education has progressed faster in its secular than
in its religious phases, the practical conclusion
is not that what we have attained is false, but
only that it is partial, and that the friends
of religion have slept when they should have
been at work. It is certainly true that the
mediæval church school and the modern secular school are opposed to each other, and if
these two were our only alternatives, our present situation would be alarming. But there
is a third alternative, and that is for religious

education itself to become modern and hence capable of taking its place alongside of and possibly also within the typical modern school. The practical measures for accomplishing this end will engage attention at a later point in our discussion. We must first of all make sure that there is no fundamental opposition of principle between religion and modern education, as, for instance, in respect to authority.

40. The Necessity of Authority in Education. The problem of authority goes to the roots of the whole idea of education. We simply cannot educate without teaching pupils to think for themselves. It is a foundation stone of the theory of teaching that the personality develops from within by the free expression of what is there, not by being compressed into a mold, or by receiving additions from without. What place is left, then, for authority? It is said that speculative anarchists, who deny altogether the right of men to govern men, sometimes carry their theory to the point of giving up all positive control of their own children. The theory is that the child will find out what is best for him through his own experience.[1] Whether

[1] Cf. article on "Some Socialist and Anarchist Views

such parents restrain the propensity of baby to put everything into his mouth is not related, but it is certain that a child could not live without restraint. It is equally certain that education consists in exercising control of some sort. Even if it does not use external compulsion, it at least arranges the conditions so as to secure reactions of one kind rather than another, and so limits the range of possible experience. It makes the child something that he would not become if he were left to himself. It chooses for him before he is able to choose for himself. We do not wait for the child to decide for himself whether he will be clean, whether he will learn to read, whether he will become acquainted with Shakespeare, with history, and with science. In both the family and the school, society genuinely predetermines the future of its new members. Authority, consequently, lies at the very basis of education both secular and religious.

41. General Nature of this Authority. What is the nature of this authority? Is it the arbitrary will of any person or group of persons? If it were that, it

 ¢ Education" in the Educational Review, Volume XV, page 1.

would be mere strength asserting itself against weakness. Parent and teacher are not the source of authority, but rather instruments of it. They themselves can be true educators only as they submit to the same authority that they exercise toward the child. Education, that is, has authority simply to make effective in child-development the laws and ideals of life that the adult finds binding upon himself. This is as true of the state as it is of the citizen. The state is simply an arrangement whereby man makes effective the obligations and ideals which he recognises as binding. It is a part of his submission to authority. In a word, it is impossible for any individual to live to himself, and for any human organization to live to itself. Child and adult alike live in and through society, and society implies authority. But society also is under the authority of some ideal of social existence which leads the way of progress. An arbitrary state is just as irrational as an arbitrary individual. It is un-human, as well as inhuman. The powers that be are all ordained as administrators of an authority which they do not originate. Religion says that they are ordained of God, and ethics cannot say less than that they are ordained by

the moral ideal. The authority that education assumes with respect to the child, then,
is identical with the authority of morals and
of religion.

42. Authority in Religious Education. In point of authorita-
tiveness, then, religious ed-
ucation stands upon the
same level as education in general and, indeed, human life in general. The real dispute, accordingly, is not between religion and
modern education, but between two conceptions of religious authority. All education
employs authority. Nevertheless, modern education humbles itself before the little child
by submitting the whole of civilisation to the
test of a fresh experience. How far the new
personality can express itself in what we regard as the true and the good, and how far it
must reject and revise and supplement what
we offer, is always an open question. Now,
the scholastic notion of authority declares
that with respect to a certain set of propositions called dogmas this question is not open.
Everywhere else the general theory of education is accepted as true, but here the principle
of development from within is no longer
trusted. An external standard is immovably
fixed, and if any individual finds that the life

within him—his conscience, his reason, his spiritual aspirations—cannot express itself in the forms of the dogma, scholastic authority must and does declare that this is a sign of a bad will. The scholastic notion of authority is not only opposed to the secular school; it is in irreconcilable conflict with modern education itself.

But there is another conception of spiritual authority which is perfectly harmonious with the educational principle of free self-expression. It holds that the immanent God utters himself in the mind of everyone of us in the form of what we call our higher self. Certainly there is that in the self which commands, judges, approves and rebukes all that is merely individual to me. My highest destiny can be nothing less or more than to become, in the highest possible degree, this better self which is germinal, yet commanding, in my consciousness. Here is divine authority, but it works within the individual as an impulse, not without him as compulsion. But there is also an external aspect to authority. For the best impulse does not grow without food; the mind does nothing and knows nothing of itself without the concurrence of an object which stimulates it to activity. We find even ourselves only through our objective experiences. Hence anything in our present civilisation or in history that actually does call out our higher nature and enable it to become dominant in us acquires thereby authority over us. Yet such authority is never merely external; it exists as authority for us only when it actually becomes the self-expression of our higher nature.[1]

Authority in this sense is not only compatible with modern education; it is essential thereto. Education in its totality is nothing more than the process whereby ideal impulse and food for it, or inner and outer authority, come most effectively together. From this point of view the question as to the authority of religion in education resolves itself into these two question: Is there a natural religious impulse, and is there in our civilisation anything that can satisfy it?[2]

[1] This is simply a general statement of the principle involved in the common Christian belief that the spiritual content of the Scriptures cannot be discovered by us without the concurrent help of the Holy Spirit. That is, external authority is not actual authority as long as it stands alone. On the other hand, it is equally true that internal authority attains a definite character for us only through contact with external fact which in some measure corresponds to it.

[2] A fuller exposition of this conception of authority in religion is contained in George A. Coe: The Religion of a Mature Mind (Chicago, 1902), Chapter III—"Authority in Religion." See also L. Laberthonnière: The Ideal Teacher: or, The Catholic Notion of Authority in Education (Cathedral Library Association, 534-536 Amsterdam

43. The Great Educational Reformers. Other characteristics of modern education will appear from a survey of the development of educational theory. The names of several educational reformers have direct significance for the problems of religious education with which we are here concerned. A mere mention of them will introduce us to our own problems, and it may stimulate some readers to secure a personal acquaintance with some of the classical literature of education.[1] Since the beginning of the Reformation a remarkable transformation has taken place. Making no effort to trace the historic continuity of its various features, we may note, first, that Luther, applying the Reformation principle of the rights of the individual, demanded compulsory education of a liberal kind for all children. The Moravian, Comenius (1502-1571; the Great Didactic, London, 1896), undertook to organise a complete course of instruction based upon the

Avenue, New York City), and J. L. Hughes: Froebel's Educational Laws for all Teachers (New York, 1899), pages 24-28.

[1] Some of the most available secondary sources of information on this topic are as follows: Thomas Davidson: History of Education (New York, 1901)—a history of both education and educational theories; R. H. Quick: Educational Reformers (New York, 1890); J. P. Munroe: The Educational Ideal (Boston, 1896); J. G. Compayré: History of Pedagogy (Boston, 1896).

principle of drawing out the faculties in the
natural order of their development, particularly by means of facts rather than books. In
France Rousseau (1712-1778; Émile, New
York, 1895), believing that the evils of life
are due chiefly to the artificiality of civilisation, demands a return to nature. This includes natural education, that is, as Rousseau
believes, development through the exercise of
spontaneous impulses, both physical and
mental. Rousseau carries this idea to mon-
strous extremes, but the idea itself, in one
form or another, has dominated the whole
modern movement. Pestalozzi (1746-1827;
Leonard and Gertrude, Boston, 1895), a
Swiss, a man of prophetic gleams but poor
organising ability, makes the school an expression of love for men, and for all men.
The end thereof is not mere learning, but also
a trained character and wholesome affections.
The method, based upon Rousseau, is chiefly
that of familiarising the child with things
rather than with words. In Germany Herbart
(1776-1841; Science of Education, Boston,
1896) defines the end of education as moral
life; shows how interest is the true spring
of study, and reveals the true nature of mental acquisition as the assimilation of new

ideas by means of those already possessed.
Froebel (1783-1852; The Education of Man,
New York, 1888), another German, founds
the kindergarten on the principles of, Pestalozzi, which he also carries forward. Free development is now the central idea. Joyous
activity takes the place of repression and external imposition. Hence play and manual
occupations receive recognition as educational
processes of the highest importance.

44. Summary of the Modern Movement in Education.   The educational movement thus barely suggested
was embedded in the political movement that has given
us the modern free state, and also in the intellectual movement that has given us modern
science. The same aspiration that gave the
franchise to the common people has endeav-
ored to liberate the child also from unnatural
burdens. The same intellectual awakening
that has given us our unprecedented knowledge of nature has also destroyed the educational monopoly that was once exercised by
books, language, and the formal part of "po-
lite learning." Bearing these general historical tendencies in mind, we shall perhaps
gather something of the profound significance
of the following summary of the modern

movement in education. (1) From being an exclusively ecclesiastical affair, education has become also an affair of the state. (2) It has ceased to be the privilege of certain classes (clergy and nobility), and has become a right of all the people. (3) Its scope has widened from mere instruction to the training of the whole person—the will, the feelings, and the body, as well as the intellect. (4) Instruction itself has broadened so as to include the study of nature and of man alongside the study of merely literary and abstractly logical subjects. (5) The material employed has changed more and more from mere symbols, such as books, formulæ, etc., toward things which the child can observe for himself. (6) The teacher's point of view has changed from that of the subject as he himself, a mature person, thinks it, to that of the child and his natural, spontaneous methods of apprehension. (7) The notion of the process has changed from that of bestowing something upon a passive child to that of providing means whereby the child may actively and freely express himself. The child is to develop from within by his own activity. (8) Finally, in these later days, as we saw in the first chapter, education has passed beyond

the individualism of both the mediæval and
the Reformation period, and is now recognised as a social process in aim as well as in
origin.

In the next chapter we shall ask what bearing certain of these views have upon religion
and education therein.

CHAPTER VI

CONTRIBUTIONS OF MODERN EDUCATION TO RELIGION

45. Why Modern Education has Neglected the Religious Factor. In a broad sense Christianity is the source of the whole movement for the reform of education. For modern schools are an offshoot from church schools, and parts of modern educational philosophy can be traced back to mediæval times. The demand for popular education and for natural methods grew up within religion, and several of the great prophets of the modern reform—notably Pestalozzi and Froebel— have looked upon it as distinctly religious. Nevertheless, education became independent. It based itself upon psychology and child-study, not upon Bible, church, or creed. It has built up a set of principles of its own without stopping to ask what bearing they may have upon religion. We have to deal, accordingly, with two apparently unrelated theories, the religious and the pedagogical, and with two independent practical activities, those of the church and those of the school.

This was, perhaps, inevitable. For religion, being the most conservative factor of civilisation, has been relatively slow in assuming a final attitude toward the rapid changes of the modern world. That the whole of education should wait for official religion to assimilate the principles of modern life was scarcely to be expected. Church and state became separated or else lost the close union of former days; modern democracy was born and grew to a giant; modern science gave us a new world. Here principles were at work that had to be incorporated into the training of the young. Progress took the line of least resistance. Leaving theological and ecclesiastical disputes to adjust themselves, the schools took into themselves the factors of life upon which there was least dispute. The reform occurred where reform was most practicable.

46. Can Religion Use the Principles of Modern Education? At last, however, this unnatural division between religion and education, church and school, is awakening a discontent that promises better things. Protestants and Catholics alike are beginning to realise that what still remains of religious education has been outstripped by the secular schools. Demand is now made not only for more religious education, but also for better, and the general assumption is that one needed step is to adopt into religious training the principles of teaching that are recognised in the state schools. Some persons believe that the reform of religious education is already going too fast in this direction. They fear that secularisation of religion will follow the adoption of methods that characterise secular schools. Now, religious education must certainly be religious in point of process as well as in point of purpose. No real advance can be made by grafting into religion anything that is not in its own nature religious. What kind of union, then, is this that is proposed? Has the educational reform any contributions whatever to make to religion? The answer to this question can be found only by analysis of the great principles underlying modern education. Let us undertake such analysis.

47. Universal Education is a Christian Idea. Universal education, to begin with, is essentially a Christian idea. For its foundation is the worth of man, a conception which Jesus has emphasised as no other teacher has done. In spite of the perversion of Christian institutions and ideas in behalf of oppression in many forms, original and es-

sential Christianity has been the great emancipator, the great protest against all exploita-
tion of human life. Rich and poor, learned
and unlearned, master and servant, king and
peasant, become, under Christian influences,
simply so many children of God and brothers
one of another. Jesus teaches that the hairs
of our heads are all numbered, that a human
life is of more value than the whole world,
and that God places so high a value upon us
as to give his only Son for our salvation.
Here is basis broad enough for democracy and
for universal education.

48. So, also, is
Development
from Within;
Modern education recog-
nises the inner life as the essential life of a man. It pro-
claims that things are not life, and that nothing can enlarge us that does not become a part
of our inner being. The school is not to hang
something upon the child, but to develop
something within him. Here, surely, is sup-
port for spiritual religion. "Out of the
heart," said a wise man of ancient times, "are
the issues of life." The Great Teacher re-
affirmed this thought again and again. Not
what comes to a man from the outside, but
what comes up out of the inner being, is the

decisive fact of life. At this point, then, Christ and modern pedagogy are at one.

49. Likewise "All-'Round Development"; Modern education not only puts emphasis upon the inner life, but it also conceives that life broadly. Life is more than knowledge; it is also appreciation of what is lovely and of good report; it is sympathy with other life; it is righteousness of purpose. To teach is more than to train the intellect and fill it with information. It is to make men. The transformation in our schools from the idea of mere instruction to that of symmetrical development is not yet fully accomplished, but in principle the victory has been won. This victory is a move in the direction of religion. For, though religion concerns the intellect, it is most of all a matter of the heart and the will. Jesus declared that he is come that we may have life, and that we may have it abundantly. There is a sense in which every true teacher could say this of himself, for he is to help his pupils, not only to know, but also to live. Whatever culture of the feelings and the will the school is able to impart is so much preparation of the soil for the reception of religious impressions.

50. And Active Self-Expression. Though modern education emphasises the inner life, it demands that this life come to outward expression. "No impression without expression" is its motto. It declares that a mental act is not complete until it has expressed itself by means of the motor apparatus, and hence that we do not really grasp an idea until we set it at work. Does not this remind us of the very words of Jesus when he said that one who hears his words without doing them is like a man who built his house on shifting sands, while he who both hears and does is like a man who built upon a rock? Entrance into the kingdom is accorded, not to those who say "Lord, Lord!" but to those who do God's will. In religion and in education alike the inner and the outer are properly indissoluble; they are the concave and the convex sides of the same curve. Hence education, working in its own way, enforces the lesson of religion. This lesson is especially significant in this day of practical affairs; for the only kind of faith that is convincing to a modern man is the faith that shows itself in its good works, the faith that spiritualises conduct, business, and all our human relations.

51. Christianity puts the Concrete before the Abstract; Another side of the same principle requires that the sensible shall come before the rational, the concrete before the abstract, the reality before the symbol. The word, the rule, the theory, is not to be introduced until the pupil has something to express by means of it. Hence, education begins, though it does not end, with things of sense. The training of the senses and of the muscles, which has become so prominent in our schools, proceeds from no unspiritual view of life, but from the actual structure of our minds. In the manual-training class the child learns vastly more than mere material things. He learns arithmetic, the laws of nature, self-control; he cultivates attention, imagination, character. A laboratory, or a landscape, or a mass of clay for modeling, if only such meanings be found therein, is fully as spiritual as a book. Modern education busies itself with objects that are visible and tangible because of what they reveal, and because of their effect upon the inner life of the child or youth. Is not this principle a principle of religion also? What is the meaning of the central idea of Christianity, incarnation, unless it be that men come into relation with

the invisible God through a visible person?
"That which we have heard, that which we
have seen with our eyes, that which we be-
held, and our hands handled, concerning the
Word of Life"—this preface of St. John's
first letter would serve with equal appropri-
ateness to introduce a fundamental conception of modern education. When this principle has its perfect work in our schools, it
will counteract two tendencies that are un-
favorable to religion—the tendency to think
of it as abstract and speculative, and the
opposite tendency to ignore the spiritual aspects of the visible world.

**52. Offers Free-
dom through
Obedience;** The educational principle
of free self-expression is
equally harmonious with re-
ligion. At first sight freedom may seem to
clash with all authority, but the apparent conflict disappears when we understand what
pedagogy means by freedom. Freedom certainly does not mean that the pupil is to do
just as he likes; for what one likes may actually repress and enslave. Unwholesome food
may be liked, but it depresses the vital powers.
Freedom is the active self-expression, not of
incidental desires, but of the deeper demands
of the nature. These deeper demands contin-

ually oppose our more superficial impulses, so that the attainment of freedom implies the learning of self-restraint and of obedience. Capricious indulgence of desire ends in slavery. We cannot be ourselves unless we train our vagrant impulses to bow before the deeper and higher things of the spirit. Freedom does not exclude authority, then, but requires it. What pedagogy insists upon under the name of freedom is simply that the teacher shall utilise the deeper currents of life so as to help the child from within rather than in any merely external fashion The deeper currents, as well as the superficial ones, will manifest themselves in spontaneous interests which it is the duty of the teacher to seize upon. Artificial leverage is to be shunned. Whatsoever is done for the child must include a spontaneous expression of the child. When, for example, restraint must be used, it should be so applied as promptly to transform itself into self-restraint.

Here, once more, modern education prepares the way for religion; for religion is itself a proclamation of liberty. Its promise is to release us from bondage to sins and fears and the pettiness of our merely individual desires. It releases us from the sense of being oppressed by the bigness of the world, and makes us realise that all things are ours, whether things present or things to come, or life or death. But it grants us this liberty only through self-surrender, only through that losing of *our* life whereby we gain *life*. In other words, religion assumes that her commands are also the commands of our own deepest self. It is thus that the obedience that we render to her is our highest freedom. Education and religion are thus at one in teaching us freedom through obedience.

53. And Trains the Individual for Society. Modern education is likewise working with religion for the adjustment of the individual to society. The demand that every child shall have opportunity for education recognises the ultimate worth of the person. It is in direct line with Christianity, which looks down through wealth, position, nationality, social circumstance, to the individual heart. On the other hand, both education and religion recognise right relations to one's fellows as a necessary part of true life. Christianity sets before us the ideal of a divine society in which each citizen loves all the others as he loves himself. Something like this is coming to be recognised as the end of education. No longer is it possible to look upon knowledge, power, intellectual and æsthetic culture, or anything else that is merely individual, as the aim of the school. The school is to make men, and strong men; but men strong in regard for one another, strong in their loyalty to law, strong in the spirit of co-operation.

54. Thus the Basis of Modern Education is Christian; These are the essential characteristics of modern educational philosophy. Every one of them is not only reconcilable with religion, but actually included within the Christian view of life. We may therefore say that *the modern educational movement as a whole has consisted in the working out of certain pedagogical aspects of Christian belief.* It has by no means appreciated all the wealth of educational principle that is contained in Christianity, nor has it always kept itself free from un-Christian tendencies of the times. Educators have often been unconscious of their indebtedness to religion; now and then one of them has been hostile to the church. Doubtless, too, the administration of education has improved less rapidly than educational theory. Yet, for all that, the educational movement of modern times has never been really independent of religion. It has builded better than it knew, for its inspiration has come from the highest source. As far as it goes, the school is essentially a creation of the religious spirit, and its work is essentially religious and Christian.

55. And its Methods are Adapted to Education in Religion. It follows that the entire body of modern educational principle is adapted to the specific work of training in religion. The spirit of modern education was received from religion, and now, enriched by new knowledge and wrought into a system, it returns to its source to become the basis of a reform in the educational methods of the church itself. The contribution of modern education to religion, then, is a suitable form and method for religious education. Thus, by another route, we reach once more the insight that the essential characteristic of such education is not its method, but rather its recognition of the whole personality of the child, the whole content of civilisation, and the whole ideal of human life.

56. The Nature of Method. Now at last we are ready for a more extended exposition of the chief principles that underlie sound method. Methods are no longer to be thought of as mere catches or devices for holding the pupil's interest while we pour ideas into his passive or neutral mind. Ingenuity is, of course, of real value to a teacher, for the teaching process can never be a merely mechanical cutting of cloth according to a pattern. But ingenuity should be in the service of insight. In the absence of educational principles, mere devices soon degenerate into vices. Sound methods grow directly out of the inmost nature of the child and of the world in which he is to realise himself. They are simply expressions of the nature of reality; they are the laws of the child's self-realisation making themselves effective through us who teach.

CHAPTER VII

EDUCATION AS DEVELOPMENT OF LIVING BEINGS

57. The Mechanical, the Vital, and the Personal. Our definition of education says that it is an effort to assist development. It consists in exercising influence upon a living being. Now, the effect of any influence depends not merely upon the source, direction, and intent of it, but also upon the kind of object upon which it is directed. We influence mere things through pushes and pulls, but a vital process cannot be controlled in quite the same way. In education we have to do with life, not with mere things. We can build a house by laying one brick upon another, but we can increase the weight of a living organism only by feeding. We can bring an organism to maturity only as an inner principle of growth makes use of the conditions which we provide. Whatever be the ultimate nature of vital processes, this practical difference between them and mechanical processes has always to be observed. A living thing grows only by assimilating food. Education, then, because it has to do with the growth of living beings, cannot be any mere mechanical compulsion, any mere moulding of material, any mere heaping up or storing of anything whatever. Its type must be feeding, not pushing and pulling, not mere adding and subtracting. It succeeds only as external material is transformed into living tissue, and this act of transforming is performed by the organism itself. Education is not a mechanical but a vital process.

Further, it is not only vital, but also personal. To be a person is not merely to act from a law that is within, and to impose this law upon external material; it is also to take possession of the law, to be a lawgiver to one's self, and so to have self-knowledge and exercise self-control. A mere thing has no self; a plant or animal has no self; for they never take possession of themselves, and their acts are never their own in this deep sense, but rather processes wrought upon or through rather than by them. Now, education seeks to influence action that is already self-action, or in process of becoming such. It is a relation between persons. Reserving for the next chapter an analysis of the personal aspect of development, let us see what is involved in the organic or vital aspect thereof.

58. The Psycho-Physical Organism. A human being is neither a lump of matter, nor a ghost, nor one of these plus the other. Man is neither a body that feels and thinks, nor yet a soul that merely uses the body as a dwelling place or as a tool. Pythagoras and Plato looked upon the body as a prison of the soul, and many Christian writers followed their example. Their view has a partial, but only partial, justification. Incitements to sin and vice arise largely out of what is called animal impulse and instinct, and in many other ways the body appears as an obstacle to the soul. Apparently it is the body that grows weary and demands sleep, that grows hungry and demands food, that contracts disease, that holds us bound to place and circumstance. Certainly it is true that bodily conditions represent to us our mental limitations, and that the attainment of good character consists in no small measure in securing control of the body for moral ends. Yet mind and body are not two utterly foreign powers. The mind does not merely conquer the body. The relation is far more intimate and positive than that. In a sense man is both body and mind; the one life has two aspects. Something like this thought appears to have been in Paul's mind when, in his discussion of the resurrection, he attributed bodily life to us even in the future world.[1] So far is the body from being a prison, or a residence, or a mere tool, that for the practical purposes of education we are obliged to look upon the physical life and the mental life as one life.[2] In psychology this relation bears the name of the co-ordination or parallelism of mind and brain. All mental activity is accompanied by brain activity; the attributes of the human mind appear in connection with a human brain, and there only; maturity of mental life must wait for maturity of body; mental health and disease have as their reverse side corresponding brain states. Even this is only the beginning of the story. We shall see in the sequel not only that the conditions of bodily growth are also conditions of mental development, but also that the specific training of character takes place partly in and through specific training of the body.[3]

[1] I Cor. 15, 35-49.

[2] Our purpose at this point is simply to secure a practical working view of the facts. The metaphysical problem has been touched upon in Chapter III, § 26.

[3] A recent writer has shown that many character-defects have a little-suspected physiological ground. Thus, a boy who indulges in 'foul' playing in basket-ball employs this underhand means very likely because he is not physically capable of winning, or of doing his part toward winning, in the normal manner. His physical

59. How the Child Gives Laws for Education. From the vital aspect of education it follows that educational laws do not originate altogether with the teacher and merely find their application in the child; in large part they originate in the child and find their point of application in the teacher. In a true sense, the child gives laws, and the teacher obeys. As a gardener is governed by the vital laws of the rose bush or cherry tree that he would cultivate, so it is with the teacher. As far as the child's body is concerned, this principle is obvious, but how few of us realise its application to the child's mind! The child or the youth perceives, feels, and thinks in his own way, and that way is different from ours. His mental development depends upon his having mental food appropriate to these mental traits. The educator's duty is to find out what kind of food is appropriate, and, having provided it, to rely upon the internal processes of assimilation to do the rest. This implies effort to discover how each thing in the child's life appears from the

vitality is likely to be found below the normal.—See article by Elias G. Brown in Boyhood, 1903 : "Curable Physical Defects," etc.—There is, in fact, scarcely a defect of disposition or of habitual will in a child or youth concerning which it is not wise to ask how far, if at all, physical conditions contribute to it.

child's own standpoint; it implies, also, imagination and sympathy, which alone make it possible for an adult to enter into child life in any living way.

What self-control and self-restraint does not this require! How easy it is to assume that what is obvious to us ought to be obvious to the young also; how laborious to ask ourselves each time how it seems from their point of view. How easy it seems for our strength to compel weak childhood to adapt itself to us and to things as they appear to us. Yet in reality we can no more compel a child's mind than we can compel his digestion. Within limits, to be sure, we can control both, but wholesome control in either case consists in providing appropriate food and other con· ditions. It consists in our obeying rather than compelling. Even when a child outwardly conforms to us; when lips repeat what we wish to hear; when the child is sincere in his utterances, there may be mental indigestion and mal-assimilation. By and by, when some catastrophe to faith or character occurs, we wonder how it is that a person who has enjoyed such a good bringing up can go so far astray. The root of the matter is that, from the beginning, pressure has taken the

place of food, and the resulting conformity
has been mistaken for growth. In other cases
we are puzzled to behold good character blossoming in a bed of weeds. The child's training has been neglected, yet he turns out well.
In such cases, if we could see all the conditions, we should generally discover that, in
some way, the child had actually had access
to appropriate food.[1]

60. The Child is not a Diminutive Adult, but Qualitatively Different. A difference between
child life and adult life has
always been recognised, of
course. But the points of
difference have not generally been understood. Our first thought is that the child
is simply small and weak, that the difference between him and a grown person
is merely quantitative. But this is not
true of either mind or body. The adult
body is not only larger and stronger; it
has also functions that are altogether absent
in the child. So it is with the mind. There is
not only a difference in range of experience
and power of inference, but also in emotional
color, in felt values, in personal meaning in
things and ideas. An adult and a child who

[1] Yet we must never assume that circumstances alone
determine character. See the next chapter, especially
§ 67.

are placed in the same situation do not necessarily experience it *as* the same, any more
than an artist and a plowman feel a given
landscape in the same way. A subjective
principle enters into the interpretation in
every case, and childhood and youth at their
various stages have characteristic modes of
interpretation. The language of religion and
morals does not mean just the same in the
mouth of a child as in that of an adult. A
given act, also, that indicates a certain mental
condition in adult life may be performed by
a child from an entirely different internal
impulse. Some of the evidence for this proposition will be given as we proceed, but all
child study proves it. The child lives in his
own world, and, though he may be truly religious, he will be so in his own way. He
should not be expected to reproduce the religion of his elders, even in diminutive form.

61. Development is More than Mere Growth. Another way of stating
this important difference
between the child and the
adult is this: The child develops, and development is more than mere growth. Growth
signifies increase in size or strength, while
development includes the further notion of
qualitative change. The normal progress of

a child is not movement up an inclined plane;
there is not simply more and more of the
same thing. We have not simply to provide
a certain kind of food in larger and larger
quantities. The problem of education is
vastly more complicated than that. The diet
of the mind, as well as that of the body, has
to be changed from time to time. The practical outcome is that we must begin to observe
times and seasons in child development. We
must know when to change from one kind of
food to another. The resulting conception is
that of a series of stages which have much
in common, but each of which makes its own
demands and its own contributions to the
child's progress.

62. Education is More than Mere Instruction. Development, rather than
instruction, is therefore the
central idea in education.
Instruction has reference to the intellect, or
function of knowing, while education has reference to the whole living being. Moreover,
instruction is not necessarily educative at all;
for it may issue in increase of knowledge
without any increase of the self. Instruction
is truly educative only when it contributes to
self development, only when it enters into
vital and nutritive connection with the child's

life from stage to stage, only when the knowledge that it conveys ceases to be an external possession and becomes, so to speak, flesh of one's flesh. The best thing that can happen to any child is to have the means of living his own life completely at each stage. That is the best preparation for the future, and nothing, absolutely nothing, is gained by attaching information to the outside of his life. Of course, a truth may have lower and higher aspects; it may even be adapted to all stages of development; and in general such truths are the most educative of all. Yet the higher aspects must await the coming of the child. To unfold them too early is to make them external and to run the risk that this external look of them will exclude all further consideration, even at the appropriate age.

63. Adaptation is More than Mere Simplification. These remarks have immediate application to religious education. For our ancient and inveterate habit has been, first, to regard the child as simply a diminutive adult; second, to identify religious instruction with religious education; and, third, to assume that the mere simplification of such instruction constitutes adequate adaptation. For adults there has been a longer catechism, and for children the same catechism abbreviated. Adaptation to childhood has been, in fact, largely verbal, as though the child could really take in a system of theology if only the words and sentences were short and simple. That this is no exaggeration of the practically universal attitude of only a few years ago could easily be proved from printed matter intended for use with children. Connected with this misunderstanding of the child was a misunderstanding of the adult also, for the assumption was made that the graces of the Christian life are in general products of a knowledge of Christian doctrines. Undoubtedly a completed character is one in which the truth is consciously realised in conduct. But this rational element is certainly not the most prominent factor even with adults, much less with children. Other elements of character appear first, such as right feeling, aspiration, habit. These things grow through processes that are unconscious to the child, and often to parents and teachers. Unconscious imitation and unreasoned adoption of prevailing standards are far more influential than any possible teaching of doctrine.

Adaptation to the child, therefore, does not consist chiefly in the simplification of language or even of ideas. It does not consist chiefly in any scheme of instruction whatever. It implies, first of all, that the whole environment of the child be attended to. His education, for weal or for woe, goes forward through everything with which he comes into contact. Food, sanitary conditions, contact with nature, with books, with newspapers, with pictures, the tone of the family life, the principles that actually control the conduct of those about him—all these must be included in any broad scheme of adaptation. Then will be added adaptation in respect to instruction. This will include, in addition to simplification, the adjustment of the subject-matter itself to the various stages of development, and the adjustment of method to the characteristic mental standpoint at each stage.

64. Spontaneous Interests as Clue and Leverage. What, then, is the clue to the actual state of the child's mind? In general, his spontaneous interests. Not all his interests, for it is possible to work up artificial ones. By means of rewards and punishments, by appeals to vanity, emulation or selfishness, by stimulation of various kinds, even the stimulus of love for a teacher, the child may be made eagerly to run in a road other than that of normal development. The mere fact that a child is interested in a study does not prove that the study is wholesome for him or that the method is sound. The interest may be a destroying fever, or, if not positively deleterious, it may over-develop the mind in one direction while essential powers are going to decay. What the child's nature actually calls for at any stage can be discovered only by noting what he spontaneously does in the presence of abundant material for self-expression. The child is essentially active in both body and mind. Watch him when he has perfect freedom, and you shall discover that work, both mental and physical, is done with enjoyment. Through such work comes power, development, education. Here the child reveals himself, and here parent and teacher find the true educational leverage. They have the task of providing truly educative material in which the pupil's interest will be spontaneous, not forced or over-stimulated.

Here is a boy who insists upon taking the family clock to pieces in order to see how it keeps time. This spontaneous interest may be treated in either of three ways: It may be suppressed, or it may be indulged without guidance, or it may be guided toward an educational end. To suppress it is to cause a wholesome intellectual impulse to wither. To indulge it without guidance leads to destructiveness and sensationalism—things will be taken to pieces for the sake of the immediate impression. But through wise feeding of this interest the boy may attain not only to knowledge of mechanical principles and devices, but also to habits of observation and sound induction.

Note, similarly, the restless hands of the boys in yonder Sunday-school class. Here is a sign that occupation should be provided for hands as well as brain, and that body and mind should work together in the learning of the day's lesson.

Here is a child who calls for stories, stories, without end. Of what possible use would it be to give such a child instruction in a doctrinal catechism? Let the spontaneous interest be fed, yet not for the sake of quieting the child. For the content of the story educates. Imagination, feeling, moral and spiritual aspiration can be called out by simply bringing appropriate images before the mind in the story form.

When a boy reaches the age that calls for "blood and thunder" stories, what shall be

done? Shall we condemn his taste because
we ourselves have outgrown it? Shall we try
to suppress such reading? That would give
incentive for the clandestine reading that has
helped to ruin many a boy. Secret disobedi-
ence is the natural result of trying to suppress a spontaneous interest. And even if
our negative measures succeed, what do we
accomplish? We simply take something of
the spirit, the freshness, the initiative out
of the boy; he is in the way of becoming
namby-pamby. The only sound method is to
supply the demand by providing wholesome
tales of adventure and heroism.[1]

65. Securing and Holding Attention. The problem of securing
and holding attention has
bothered teachers always
and everywhere. One reason therefor is that
the relation of attention to interest has been
only imperfectly understood. On this point
there are two extremes to be avoided. One is
the old notion of compelling attention by
creating artificial interests, whether by means
of rewards and punishments, or by means of
emulation or other kinds of artificial stimula-

---

[1] At the same time, we should remember that an interest that appears to be spontaneous may be a product
of earlier training or of earlier neglect. See Introduc-
tion to Irving King: The Psychology of Child-Development (Chicago, 1903).

tion. The other extreme consists in relying so completely upon spontaneous, pleasure-giving interests as not to produce the absolutely essential habit of giving attention to disagreeable things. If we adopt the first extreme, the artificiality of the incentives upon which we rely is likely to be attributed by the pupil to the subject-matter of instruction. But if we adopt the second extreme, our pupils will fail to learn the lesson of doing duty as good soldiers, whether it is agreeable or not.

The child must be trained, then, to attend to unattractive things, yet not as a slave under compulsion, but through an inner, personal interest in them. This is to say that the range and depth of his interests must be increased. The entering wedge is the present, spontaneous interest, whatever it may be. This already has the attention. The next move is to feed this interest with such material as enlarges and guides it, and so transfers attention to new matter which at first perhaps is not felt to be interesting. Interest in things present can be extended to things of the same class in the past. From picture to story, from story to biography, from biography to history; from a battle as an outward event to the issue involved, and finally to political or ethical principles; from our national heroes to the heroes of the Bible and of Christian history—these will represent the principle of extending interests and so extending attention. In general, attention should be secured and held through the intrinsic value which the child feels to be present in the subject-matter of instruction. This does not exclude such extrinsic incitements as arise naturally through group activities, but it warns us against detaching instruction from the immediate, spontaneous interest. On the basis of intrinsic interest the teacher can secure the hardest work, work that even approximates the hardships that children willingly go through in carrying on their sports or other self-initiated enterprises. Furthermore, self-imposed hard work, if the subject-matter be worthy and of sufficient breadth and depth, is the most educative. For in later life the real test of our character will be whether we will impose upon ourselves tasks that we might escape, whether we will *take* an interest in that which is worthy of our interest.[1]

[1] On the relation of spontaneous to acquired interests, see William James: Talks to Teachers on Psychology (New York, 1899). On the necessity of starting all instruction at the child's level and upon the ground of an already existing interest, see Patterson DuBois: The Point of Contact in Teaching (New York, 1901).

66. Apperception or Mental Assimilation. This principle of building from within outward must be pursued a step further. A spontaneous interest means that the mind is actively seeking its food. Now, just as physical food, in order to fulfil its end, must be not only eaten but also assimilated, so instruction must be mentally assimilated before it can build up the mind.[1] The technical name for mental assimilation is apperception. The fact is as simple as the name is clumsy. The essential fact is that we understand a new idea by means of ideas we already have. A little boy who had learned to call a dog "bow-wow," gave the same name to cats, sheep, and other small animals. When the Thanksgiving turkey appeared upon the table, "Bow-wow" was his remark. Similarly cows and other large animals were called "ossy" (horse). This extension of old names to new objects is an outward sign that new objects are being grouped into the classes already recognised. The new is thus being assimilated by means of the old. In the days before the Chicago River had been purified by means of the drainage canal, a little girl was heard to

[1] To this physical simile, Patterson DuBois has added several others, as nurture by atmosphere, by light, and by exercise.—The Natural Way in Moral Training (New York, 1903).

remark to a companion, "I hate rivers, don't you?" "Why?" said the other. "Because they smell so!" was the reply. This little girl was interpreting her instruction in geography by means of her own experiences.

This process is a universal one. We see the new through the old, the distant through the near; we understand things that we have not experienced by imaging them under the form of those that we have experienced. We grasp the idea of God's love through our experience as children and parents, or as wives and husbands, and the highest conception of divinity that we can form is that which we receive through contemplation of a complete human life. On the other hand, each new experience or idea, in the act of being interpreted by means of an old one, modifies it. After the little boy had called the Thanksgiving turkey "bow-wow," this name meant more to him than before, and the object, dog, had new and wider relationships. The great fact of apperception, then, broadly stated, is that the old idea interprets the new one, but is modified by it.

The applications of this principle to education are perfectly direct. *First,* the success of any educational effort depends at every stage upon the extent and depth of the child's past experience not less than upon the new material that is presented. Hence the value of large and varied contact with nature, of handling things, of using tools, of engaging all the senses and all the active powers. *Second,* perceiving anything is more than merely seeing it, and learning a truth is more than committing to memory the formula thereof, even though the meaning of every word in the formula be understood. The ability to define and formulate, or even to give correct answers to searching questions does not measure one's actual acquisitions. The important question always is this: What does this mean to the child in terms of his own experience? *Third,* it follows that the teacher must give at least as much attention to what is already in the child's mind as to the new ideas that are to be presented. The new idea cannot be handed over, or fired into the waiting mind. It can only be attached to some idea already there, and if it is not so attached it is not really acquired. One of the great undertakings of the child-study movement is to discover what is the stock of ideas of children at various ages. Such a stock of ideas reveals "the point of contact" with the

child's actual experience, and knowledge of it
enables the teacher to effect the junction or
rather fusion of the new and the old through
the child's own spontaneous interest. Many
applications of this principle to religious and
moral instruction lie upon the surface. Others
will be unfolded as we proceed.

CHAPTER VIII

EDUCATION AS DEVELOPMENT OF PERSONS

67. What is it to be a Person? We have said that the child is not merely an organism, physical and mental, but also a person. What is it to be a person? Without being too formal or technical, we may answer that personality implies self-knowledge and self-control, or, more definitely, the ability to think one's self in relation to one's world, set ends before one's self as desirable, and freely choose them as one's own. Now, education is intended to assist the child to realise himself as a person. Here our figure of development through feeding ceases to be adequate. For, whereas digestion and assimilation are wrought within us rather than by us, we are persons only through acts of self-discrimination, self-criticism, and choice that are strictly our own. There is a sense in which personality or selfhood may be said to be self-attained rather than bestowed. From within are the issues of life. Of course we are not self-originating but created, yet the deepest mystery of creation lies just in the fact that we are at once dependent creatures and yet free persons, that we are bestowed upon ourselves and yet have to attain to ourselves. At the beginning of life we are free persons only in a potential sense. We are not in possession of ourselves, but we are possessed by impressions and impulses. In a very complete sense we are as yet creatures of circumstances. Only through a long and slow process of education does anyone attain to his own self, but in proportion as he does attain thereunto he becomes free. He is no longer a mere mental mechanism moved by blind impulse, but in some measure he uses the mechanism of his own mind for self-chosen ends. He is no longer a mere creature of circumstances; he does not merely adjust himself to his environment, but rather he adjusts his environment to his own ends. What a circumstance shall be to a person depends upon what the person chooses to make of it.[1] In view of all this we may well modify our earlier definitions of education by making it to be an effort to assist immature persons to realise themselves and their destiny as persons.

[1] Mackenzie well says that what a circumstance is to us, and so what are to be reckoned circumstances, depends upon our character. The same external or internal fact is one thing to one man, another to another.—J. S. Mackenzie: Manual of Ethics (London, 1899), pages 85 ff.

68. Self-Realisation Requires Self-Expression. Education is to assist self-realisation. This implies, first, that the pupil is to be active, not passive. It implies, in the second place, not only activity, or the exercise of functions, but also self-originating activity. In a sense the only education possible for a person is self-education. This is not quite the same as training. Training includes the formation of habit and increase of power or accuracy through practice; education includes all this and in addition the securing possession of one's self or free self-realisation. A dog or a horse can be trained, but only persons can be educated. It follows, in the third place, that true education must develop individuality. Its products cannot be machine-made and uniform. It is true, as Jesus tells us, that we can save our life only by self-sacrifice for society, but there must first be a self before there can be self-sacrifice. The self-sacrifice that Jesus had in mind is not dull conformity or obliteration of individuality, but the active contribution to society of something that is worth while. The more distinctive the contribution, the more does it enrich the life of society. The social end of education is therefore *not* hindered but promoted through the development of strong individuality in pupils.[1] Summing up these implicates, we may say that the education of persons must assist their self-realisation, that self-realisation requires self-expression, and that this includes activity, initiative or freedom, and individuality.

69. "No Impression without Expression." The necessity for activity on the part of the pupil might have been shown in the last chapter, where we were dealing with the mind simply as an organism. For growth, as everyone knows, comes through exercise. But this truth attains vastly deeper meaning through its connection with the principle of personal self-realisation. With the thought of personality in the background we now proceed to examine the general relation of activity to mental development. The necessity of pupil-activity in education has attained crystalline expression in two maxims or mottoes: "No impression without expression," and "Learn by doing." The first of these maxims means that everything received by the pupil from teacher or text-book must

---

[1] For a discussion of the social aspect of religious education, see Chapter XXII.

be expressed by the pupil before it can become a vital possession. We do not really learn anything until we express it in word or act. We do not first learn it and then express it, but the expression is itself a part of the process of acquisition. Impression without expression leaves the mind at best in a state of apparent but unreal illumination. Anyone can observe this in himself. How often do we fancy that we have grasped a subject, only to find the merest ghosts of ideas in our mind when we try to *tell* what we suppose we know or believe. How many times, too, have we seen our subject develop and grow clear in the *act* of talking or writing about it. How much more so is it with children, whose resources are so much less than ours. Impression must pass promptly over into expression, or become powerless and meaningless. The very little child must tell the story in his own words, or act it out; older children must recite the lesson, or write a composition, or draw a map or picture, or work out a problem, or devise a dramatic representation. Such modes of expression are not over and above the work of instruction, but an essential part of it.

70. An Illustration. A teacher in a public school was instructing her pupils in the history of our country. The lesson for the day was the landing of the Pilgrims at Plymouth. The story was first told, and then the teacher said, ''Would you like to play this story?'' The children assented, and a leader, a little girl, was appointed. She promptly called out other children and assigned them their parts, and without hint or guidance from any source she devised and the children enacted the following scene: The Mayflower was represented by children arranged in two lines like those of a ship's sides. At bow and at stern a child held a flag. The Pilgrims were represented by the other children, who were first enclosed within the lines just referred to, and later walked ashore with due gravity. The value of such an exercise is manifold. It makes the story vivid to the pupil, gives it reality, fixes it in the memory, and—what is at least equally important—develops initiative and individuality.

71. ''Learn by Doing.'' We shall see, after a while, how the motto, ''No impression without expression,'' is being applied in Sunday-school instruction. But first we must unfold the general principle a little further. "Learn by doing" advances us another step. This maxim means that an idea is best acquired by doing something in which the idea is used. Children, as everybody knows, like to do things. Now, the modern teacher takes advantage of this fact by leading the child to do things in which there arises need for measurement (which involves arithmetic), language (reading and writing), geographical and historical knowledge, etc. The most advanced experiment in this direction is that of Professor John Dewey, who has organised a school in which the child is to be led by this method from the earliest kindergarten age to his entrance to college.[1] One purpose of this school is to continue the natural education that is begun in the family by the contact of the child with life in the concrete. The pupil accordingly engages in three domestic occupations that are fundamental to human well-being—the preparation of food (cooking), of clothing (spinning and weaving), and of shelter (carpentry, etc.). This work introduces him at once to nature, and he acquires some of the rudiments of natural and physical science. Since it requires measurement, symbols, and records, he is led to

[1] See John Dewey: The School and Society (Chicago, 1900).

feel the need of arithmetic, reading and writing, and he studies them in response to his
own spontaneous interest, and for the sake of
their immediate usableness. The simpler
forms of these three occupations are first undertaken, then the more complex. As this
sequence reproduces the order of the development of civilisation, the pupil becomes interested in history; he lives it through, to some
extent, in miniature. At every step his in-
ventive or creative power is given scope,
whether in practical or artistic form. At
every step, too, the work is co-operative, and
therefore educative of the social feelings. The
bearing of this remarkable experiment is complex, yet certain principles stand out clearly.
For one thing, the child is dealing with real
life, so that the ordinary artificial isolation of
the school from the home and from the world's
work is avoided. Then, always appealing to
the pupil's spontaneous interest, the school
arranges the material and the occupations so
that the resulting reactions adjust the individual to his fellows, and to the knowledge,
the arts, and the industries by which society
lives. The point for our especial attention,
however, is the radical way in which the principle of learning by doing is applied. Just as

the race has come by its knowledge primarily through doing the things necessary for preserving life and attaining life's chosen ends, so the child is to be instructed by doing the things in which he, too, is really interested.

72. The Sensori-Motor Arc. The necessity for education through the pupil's activity is grounded in our nervous and mental structure. Looked at broadly, the work of mind consists in transforming impressions into acts. The nervous mechanism involved in this process is technically described as the "sensori-motor arc." The chief parts of our nervous system are three: sensory nerves, which conduct sense-stimulus to the brain; the brain itself, which serves as a sort of central telephone exchange for putting one part of the organism into touch with other parts; and the motor nerves, which conduct the stimulus of motion to the muscles and cause them to contract. Similarly, our typical conscious states are first, impressions of sense; second, our thoughts and emotions; and, third, our volitions and impulses to action. At first sight we fancy that these three come in serial order, first impression, then thought, then action; but this is only half the truth. For, while thought may be deliberate, and action may be postponed to await the conclusion of reflection, nevertheless no one of these processes ever takes place entirely by itself. A complete mental state involves all three aspects of mind. With every impression there goes at least a nascent act. At the very least there are changes in the circulation and the breathing, and even our voluntary muscles contract and relax in greater or less degree with the changing shades of mental impression. Anyone can easily prove this to himself by occasionally taking note of the state of the physical organism when the mind appears to be merely receiving impressions, as in listening to a story, looking at a landscape, etc. The point of all this, as far as education is concerned, is that a mental state is never complete until it has adequate expression, or until act balances impression. Whatever clogs the active or expressive channels clogs the whole flow of mental energy. The result of inadequate expression is unclearness, misunderstanding, forgetfulness, or possibly a superficial conceit of knowledge.

73. Neglect of Expression in Religious Training. This principle holds for adults as well as for children, and neglect of it accounts for many a failure,

complete or partial, in religious work.
Preaching, for example, is often weak, in spite
of both intelligence and earnestness, because
it fails to reveal a direct way for the hearers
actively to apply the truth they hear. An
effective sermon is not necessarily the same
as an affecting one. The pew must talk and
act before the impression made by the pulpit
can be a really vital matter, and the talking
and acting, let it be remembered, are not mere
consequences of having the truth, but also a
part of the process of getting hold of it. "If
any man wills to do . . . he shall know." If
this be true of church work with adults, how
much more does it apply to work with
children? Adults have many modes of self-
expression, some of which are indirect, and
many of which can be postponed to a greater
or less extent. But a child must express himself at once and directly, or the impression
fades beyond effective recovery.

In many cases church methods with the
young are very little more than a weakened
form of preaching. They ignore the necessity
of active expression. This is one of the reasons
why biblical facts and spiritual truths remain
so external to many pupils of the Sunday
school. Biblical history that is gone over and

over in the class is forgotten, and the child reaches maturity shockingly ignorant of the simplest facts. One ignorant saint who puts the Bible to daily use, and so expresses his impressions, learns more of the Scriptures in a year than many a bright Sunday-school pupil learns in a double seven year cycle. The same principle applies to the "applications" or "lessons" to be gathered from the biblical material. Many teachers fancy that their most important duty is to tell the class just what moral or spiritual lesson can be learned from the passage under consideration. But if a teacher stops here he is likely to do more harm than good. A religious impression that does not secure expression is worse than no impression at all. For it remains external, it seems unreal, and the repetition of such religious impressions leads finally to a habit of regarding religion itself as external and unrelated to one's real life.

74. Not only Activity, but Also Free Self-Activity. Let us now see the bearing of all this upon personality, an idea which for the moment has been kept in the background. We have seen that the child should express whatever he is set to learn, and that this expression takes place most nor-

mally when the facts or truths to be mastered
occur to him as essential parts of some active
work in which he is spontaneously interested.
A third and deeper aspect of the case is that
the pupil here takes the initiative and in the
outcome expresses not merely the fact or truth
that he is learning, but also *himself*. Pestalozzi laid the stress upon activity, but Froebel
upon self-activity.[1] That is, the child enters
upon a given educational activity because of
his own interest in that activity. In a sense,
he freely initiates and carries forward his own
education. While the teacher chooses for him
by providing certain kinds of material for
self-expression rather than others, the child
also chooses for himself because he is interested in that material. His reactions upon it
constitute his own free self-expression. He
not merely learns something, he also progres-
sively discovers himself. If it were possible
for him to put this aspect of his experience
into words, he might say: "I discover that,
to live my very own life, I must say 'I am,'
not 'I is'; that I must be able to know how
much one-third of one-half is; that I must
know the boundaries of my town, my county,
my state; that I must realise where my food

[1] J. L. Hughes: Froebel's Educational Laws for all
Teachers (New York, 1899), Chapters IX and X.

comes from, how my ancestors attained civilised life and conquered their liberty. All these things belong to me, and I should be less myself without them.''

75. Freedom in Education. This is the great principle of freedom in education. The child is not to be forced into any pre-arranged mold. He is not merely to imitate. He is not merely to assimilate food. He is rather to attain to selfhood by a series of spontaneously initiated activities that lead to a progressive series of self-discoveries. The movement for freedom in education is practically parallel with the modern movement for popular government. The two reforms are, in fact, parts of one effort of the human spirit. When the movement for American independence and for popular government in France was organising itself, the pedagogical reform was also setting in. The century of our political liberty is also the century in which the child has been emancipated from repressive school methods. Many men now living have witnessed a large part of this peaceful revolution. They can recall a time when both the instruction and the discipline in the ordinary school were full of restraint and compulsion intended to mold the child to the teacher's ideas. In the well managed school of to-day, if any child does not learn, if he is restless or refractory, the teacher, instead of concocting schemes for more effective compulsion, asks himself wherein he has failed to understand the child and adapt the school work to him.

The kindergarten has been not only the most complete expression of this idea, but also the leader of all other branches of general education. It has stood as protector of the joyous spontaneity of childhood. It has steadily asserted that when the child comes into the schoolroom he should not be expected to lay aside the freedom of his home life and his plays. He should continue freely to express himself, and the school should find its mission in providing means for fuller and richer and freer self-expression. From the kindergarten this idea has spread upward through the whole school organism even to the college. The elective system of studies has been adopted by the colleges and is being adopted by the high schools largely in response to this principle. School discipline has become largely a matter of student self-government. As a consequence, school work has become more joyous and discipline easier.

Now, joy in work leads to harder work and

larger results. Two or three generations ago
most teachers would probably have denied the
proposition that pupils like hard work. To-
day thoughtful teachers would make a distinction: children and youths like hard work
that is self-expressive, but they still dislike
the task that has no personal meaning for
them. Children are not naturally lazy. Quite
the contrary. For behold the wealth of physical and mental energy that they put into
games and the solving of puzzles. It is utterly
natural for the young to work hard, and to
gain thereby physical and mental ruggedness,
vigor, power of application. Every healthy
child or youth is a storage battery of power
that merely waits for opportunity to discharge
itself. Any pupil who is not habitually atten-
tive and interested should be assumed to be
either defective in body or mind, or else suffering the results of defective method.

76. Interest of Religion and Morals in this Principle. The interest of religion
and morals in the principle
of freedom in education is
greater, if possible, than
that of so-called secular education. For religion and morals have primary reference to the
free personality as such. Their aim is to
induce men freely to choose the good, nay,

they aim even to make men like the good and find their freedom and self-realisation therein. Religious and moral education, accordingly, cannot be anything less than the progressive attainment of freedom through the exercise of freedom; and its method can be nothing less than placing the child in a series of such concrete situations as shall reveal him to himself as really interested in the good and self-enlisted on its side. This involves growing knowledge of good and evil, a developing spiritual appreciation, and training of the will. It is not instruction alone; it is not habit alone; it is not merely instruction plus habit; it is also the personal sense of reality, of discovering one's very own life. This is true not only of the ethical side of religion, but also of the sacred experiences in which the soul realises the presence of God. Here, too, is freedom and the highest joy, and the road thereto is likewise that of free self-expression.

CHAPTER IX

PUNISHMENT AND PLAY

77. Necessary Limits of Freedom. The present chapter will be an attempt to illustrate and apply the principle of free self-expression by reference to the two extremes, play and punishment. The former appears at first sight to correspond most closely to the idea of free self-expression, yet to have little educational value, while the latter appears to contradict the principle of free self-expression, yet to be essential to training of the moral will. We will begin with punishment. This does, indeed, stand for a limitation upon freedom, but upon reflection we perceive that freedom must, in any case, be limited. Every boy, for example, wishes to play with powder and fire-arms. Now, here is a situation in which, in general, freedom cannot be and remain unlimited. For, if the parent does not say "No," the explosives themselves will say it by injuring the boy and curtailing his power. This is a typical case. Unrestrained freedom destroys freedom, and conversely the most complete

freedom is self-limiting. In the case of fire-
arms the most complete freedom is that of an
adult who, in view of the nature of explosives, voluntarily restrains or sets rules to himself.

Free self-expression, then, includes self-
restraint. Now, the problem with regard to
punishment of the young is simply whether
punishments inflicted against the will of the
child may nevertheless constitute to the child
his own self-expression in the way of self-
limitation. We know that mere habits can be
formed under the influence of prospective or
actual chastisement, and that, to this extent,
the rod may help to form the character. But,
unless in and through the chastisement the
child discovers *himself*, the value of the habits
thus formed may be seriously doubted. The
practical aim must be to make all punishments self-punishments, all restraints self-
restraints.

78. Common Mistakes as to Punishment. Children are punished
less often and less severely
than formerly. This is due
in part to increasing emphasis upon the
milder aspects of Christianity, in part
to the movement for freedom in education, and in part, perhaps, to simple dis-

inclination to take up a problem of so great
delicacy. In the main this change in the lot
of childhood is probably for the better. Yet
no one will deny that chastisement is often
inflicted unwisely, or that it is often omitted
where it is most needed. There is ground for
suspecting that few parents have any clear
notion, and fewer still any sound one, of the
relation of punishment to character building.
Penalties are inflicted for the sake of some
slight immediate end, such as quiet in the
household, or even as an act of resentment.
Punishment is frequently omitted altogether
for the sake of avoiding disturbance, or because a parent fears to create a situation
that he may not be able to control. It will not
be out of place, then, to state a few maxims
which grow directly out of the fact that our
supreme duty to the young is to assist their
development as persons.

That punishment should never be inflicted
upon children by an angry person, or because of anger, resentment, or irritation of
any kind, is almost self-evident. Whenever
it is inflicted it should be as deliberate and
well reasoned as an important business contract, and it should be administered as a duty
that may not be put aside. Further, it should

have a definite good end in view; it should
look to the future, not merely to the past.
Whatever be our conceptions of divine punishments or of state punishments, certainly in
the case of children mere retaliation, the mere
vindication of broken law, and the mere assertion of authority or of abstract justice are out
of place.   The essential question is, What
effect will the proposed treatment of the child
have upon his own development? This question cannot be answered without considering
the effect upon the spirit as well as the outward conduct. To punish wisely is to punish
the inmost self so that life shall issue out of
it.

**79. Punishment
as Self-
Expression.**
Punishment is educative
in proportion as the dis-
comfort of it seems to the
child to be a genuine expression of what he
himself is or does, so that desire awakens to
overcome the present self and rise to a higher
one. It is not enough to prevent the doing of
some things and secure the doing of others;
discipline fails unless it helps the child to
desire to do and to abstain. Correct discipline cultivates the preferences, the standard,
the sense of what one really is. In a word,
punishment should be the self-expression of

a lower self out of which arises the sense of a higher self. To this end, penalties should be natural rather than artificial, that is, they should be and seem to be direct results of the child's own act rather than impositions of an apparently arbitrary will. Children should not be shielded too much from the painful consequences of foolish conduct. There is educative value in bruises, cuts, burns, and even in scratches and blows from other children. One of the worst situations into which a child can be placed is a home that so shields him from pain that he fails to learn the fact of law, both natural and social, and the correlative fact that self-restraint is essential to the largest freedom.

Punishment in the strict sense—that is, as distinguished from mere consequences that occur under natural law—will have to do chiefly with violations of the conditions of social life. Here is where arbitrariness on the part of parent or teacher is most likely to creep in. Even rules that are really not arbitrary may seem so to the child, and punishment for infringement of them, though it be a true copy of real life, may seem to him artificial, unreasonable, and arbitrary. This is a serious matter. For whatever seems to the

child like mere arbitrariness tends to call
forth a response of the same kind; in defence
of his own sense of self, he conceals, deceives,
and devises unsocial means of self-assertion.

Rules and penalties, then, should not only
not be arbitrary; they should not seem to be
so. This will involve something in the way of
explanation, but more in the way of devising
social penalties that the offender shall see to
be self-imposed. For example, selfishness and
disregard of established order tend to break
up plays and games; therefore, in the interest
of a game or play, which is the child's own
interest, a wilful child must sometimes be
denied a desired pastime. Of course no chastisement for the moment seems joyous, but
grievous. Temporarily the disciplinarian
must oppose the child; yet the nature of the
violated rule, the nature of the penalty, and
the personal attitude in the administration
thereof should all be such that the child
quickly realises that his deeper will is in harmony with the hand that chastises. A little
boy by his play in the family living room had
endangered a lighted lamp. He was repeat-
edly warned, but the play impulse overcame
him, he forgot, and soon the lamp was over-
turned. Thereupon one of the parents, ex-

plaining to the little boy the dangers of a poor
memory, and pointing out that the little boy's
own memory needed external help, administered sharp corporeal punishment. It was
for the sake of the future, not of the past; it
represented a necessary order of things rather
than an arbitrary will; it became to the child-
consciousness at once an expression of his
imperfect self and a means of helping him to
realise a higher selfhood.[1]

80. Educational Value of Play. Let us turn now to the
extreme opposite of punish-
ment, the unrestrained freedom of play. Al-
cuin (died 804), who is usually regarded as
the father of mediæval education, looked upon
play as frivolous and worthy only of being
discouraged or suppressed. In this he was followed by various educators. Until comparatively recent times, even those who have not
condemned plays and games have nevertheless looked upon them as essentially useless,
or at best as a relatively harmless way of occupying children who are too young to be
doing anything useful. All this is now re-
versed. The plays of the young, since they

[1] See Elizabeth Harrison: A Study of Child Nature
(Chicago Kindergarten College, 1902), and Herbert Spen-
cer: Education: Intellectual, Moral, and Physical (New
York, 1872).

reveal the spontaneous interests, have become
a clue to educational problems; and since
spontaneous interest has become the leverage
of the teacher in the education of the child,
the conscious effort of teachers has been to
make the work of the schoolroom somewhat
like the work of the playground. There is no
absolute dividing line between the two kinds
of work. Nor is this all. For play itself
turns out to be a first-class educational process. The play instinct is nature's way, and
so God's way, of deveyoping body, mind and
character. Quickness and accuracy of perception; co-ordination of the muscles, which
puts the body at the prompt service of the
mind; rapidity of thought; accuracy of judgment; promptness of decision; self-control;
respect for others; the habit of co-operation;
self-sacrifice for the good of a group—all
these products of true education are called
out in plays and games. Further, the play
instinct varies with the different species and
with the two sexes, so that its specific forms
prepare the individual for his specific functions. The plays of a lamb prepare for the
activities of a grazing animal; those of a
lion's whelp foretell the pursuit and killing
of prey. The plays of a girl look forward to

motherhood; those of a boy to protecting,
building, acquiring. In short, play is a part
of nature's school.

81. Relation of Play to Religious Education. The relation of play to religious education demands a specific word. Just
as the gap between the school and play is be-
ing filled up, so the home and the church
should now at last awake to the divine significance of the play instinct and make use
of it for the purpose of developing the spiritual nature. The opposition between the play
spirit and the religious spirit is not real but
only fancied; just as that between play and
schooling in general. Through our ignorance
we have put asunder that which God hath
joined together. Here is the secret of much
of our lack of power with young people. We
teach children to think of their most free and
spontaneous activities, their plays, as having
no affinity for religion, and then we wonder
why religion does not seem more attractive to
them as they grow toward maturity! We
mask the joy and freedom of religion by our
long faces, our perfunctory devotions, our
whispers and reticences, and then we find it
strange that young people are so inordinately
fond of worldly pleasures! As late as the

year 1900 a prominent Sunday-school leader
insisted upon keeping up this paralysing distinction. "It is wrong," he said, "to talk
about the kindergarten of the Bible school.
Wise primary workers are averse to turning
any part of the Bible school into a kindergarten because the thought of play should be
kept for places other than God's house, and
for times other than the Lord's day. The
little ones should be taught reverence very
early in life." As long as such notions prevail, we should expect children to exclude
God from their plays, think of religion as
unnatural, and either grow up indifferent to
religion or else reserve their reverence for the
Lord's day and the Lord's house. Unless we
discover the unity of play with education in
religion as well as with so called secular education, we shall never secure control of the
whole child or the whole youth for Christ.

82. The Christian Interpretation of Play. The practical problem is, in part, to extend the Christian spirit through all
the games and plays of childhood and youth,
and the play spirit through the instrumental-
ities of religious education, so that the whole
life shall be lived as in the sight of God and
in friendship with Christ. If the thought of

God or of Christ chills the joy of games and
plays, that merely proves that we have mis-
interpreted the divine to children. A child
who cannot freely unbend in the presence of
his earthly father or an elder brother is a
witness against such a father or such a
brother. There is imperfectly revealed
fatherhood, and imperfectly revealed brother-
hood. The fact that we have so represented
the Heavenly Father and the great Elder
Brother of us all shows how slow of heart we
have been, how slightly we have grasped the
principle of incarnation. God in Christ
means God in childhood as well as in manhood; God in childhood's plays, therefore,
as truly as in manhood's labor and worship.
In fact, the freedom of play is a normal element of life and a normal attitude toward
life for adults as well as children. Bushnell
says: "Play is the symbol and interpreter of
liberty, that is, Christian liberty. * * *
Play wants no motive but play; and so true
goodness, when it is ripe in the soul and is
become a complete inspiration there, will ask
no motive but to be good. Therefore God has
purposely set the beginning of the natural
life in a mood that foreshadows the last and
highest chapter of immortal character." Thus

play becomes " a natural interpreter of what is highest and last in the grand problem of our life itself." [1]

Holding this view of play, we should strive, not to make children like playless adults, but to make adults like playful children. Throughout education the play attitude of mind should be preserved as far as possible. After all, is it not right jolly to learn things, to have an occupation, to do something worth while? Is it not fun to do right? True, there are unavoidable crosses; there is weakness where we would have strength; there is waiting when we wish to act, action when we wish to rest; there are deprivation and sorrow, and always the demand for self-sacrifice. Yet Jesus made no mistake when he called the yoke easy and the burden light, and Paul was right when he called the law of Christ a law of liberty. For children and adults alike Christ is the great emancipator, the great restorer of the play spirit. Through him there is rejoicing, even in tribulation; through him the meanest duty becomes a divine mission; through him the human being for the first time clearly realises that he is a child of God, with a child's prerogatives. Why, then, are

[1] Horace Bushnell: Christian Nurture (New York: Scribners), Part II, Ch. VI, pages 339 f.

we so sober in our daily occupations, so unable to relax into the childlike state of mind? Because we think too meanly of our life; because of our narrow self-consciousness; because the larger self is denied a chance for full utterance. If we would enter into the fulness of life we must become as little children, and we must remain so. Applying this principle to the education of children, we should strive to prevent even the semblance of a break between the playground, the family altar, and the church.

83. Christ as Master of the Playground. This will necessitate such supervision of children's plays as will make Christ the master of the playground—the master, not the spy or the oppressor; the promoter, not the opponent of play. What a shame it is that he has been represented to children as mere restraint, a mere ''don't,'' a negation, whereas he is come that children may have their own life and that they may have it abundantly. That means play, with its fun, its noise, its contests. The more of Christ there is in play, the more fun there is; for the things that Christ forbids, which center in undue self-love, are the very things that destroy play, while the things that he com-

mands, which center in social or group activities, are the very things that keep play
going at its highest. This does not mean that
Christ would have goody-goody boys and
girls. Boisterousness, struggle, conquest, the
taking of risks and the facing of danger—all
these are at some time proper and truly
Christian. We must always remember that
"is" and "is not" are not the only alternatives; there is also "becoming." The essential question is never, Does this child fulfil
the law of love? but rather, Is he advancing
normally toward a mature realisation and
fulfilment of it?

The normal way for children to make this
advance is to live out their childish selves in
association with one another. They are to
live, but they are also to live together. Their
contests, even their quarrels, are of value.
Quarrels among children are not to be interpreted as signs of a fall from virtue, but
rather as thorns with which the child pricks
himself in his efforts to pluck the rose of
normal social existence. Childhood quarrels
provide one with a set of experiences that enable one to avoid quarreling later in life.
When grown persons indulge wrath and
envy and backbiting and clamoring, they de-

scend from a plane that the child has not yet
reached, a plane that his early social experience helps him to reach.

Thus an act which in an adult is bad is not
necessarily so in a child. Christ comes to
children's quarrels, not to condemn them, but
so to illuminate them as to make them self-
rebuking and self-annihilating. To suppress
them by mere power is to sacrifice development. They are essentially self-destroying,
and this is the very lesson that the child
learns from them. The same may be said of
children's anger. It is a stage of undeveloped life. Anger must be experienced before
character can become rugged. He who knows
not anger knows not how to fight the wrong.
So, also, of childhood greed and self-assertive-
ness. These impulses, if allowed to grow
without check, become in time an evil character. But they should develop into strength
of personality, power of resistance, power to
do and to win in worthy causes. To make
Christ master of the playground, then, means
such wise and subtle supervision of play as
helps childhood impulses gradually to interpret themselves through their own expression
into the Christian philosophy of life.

CHAPTER X

84. The Divine Method of Educating the Race. In our discussion of apperception and of self-activity we caught a glimpse of some practical applications of a principle, already formulated in Chapter VI, concerning the superior educational value of concrete realities and actual experiences as compared with that of words or other symbols. This principle now demands specific attention. If we ask ourselves by what method the divine education of the race from savagery to civilisation has proceeded, we shall be struck at once with the fact that God seems to have hidden himself behind the visible and tangible environment of human life. The race has escaped from savagery through its own self activity, namely, through the wrestlings of men with nature and with one another. Thus concrete things and visible persons have been the primary instruments of man's training. Out of the tussle with wild beasts, with the rigors of winter, with hostile tribes, with all the conditions of physical existence, came quickened faculties, useful customs and instincts, and a stock of experience that was destined to unfold into science, literature, art, and politics.

This is the case with morals and religion as well as with the other elements of civilisation. In neither of these spheres was the race started into life equipped with ready-made ideas or formulas, or with any short-cut method of acquiring them. Moral and religious ideas and feelings gradually unfolded themselves through what seems, from our point of view, like a haphazard, rough and tumble, and very unspiritual struggle to live. Yet the education of the race was actually beginning. Its method was, first the sensible, then the rational; first the concrete, then the abstract; first the experience, then the symbol. This order will be found to hold at every stage of race education. That great body of symbols, the Bible, for example, came gradually into existence as the recorded expression of the growing religious experience of the chosen people. It is not the source of that experience, but a product of it, though each part of the Scriptures, once in existence, entered as a factor into the movement whence it sprung. Yet the mere symbol, of whatever kind it may, be, and however useful in communicating the results of experience, can never quite take the place of the concrete fact. We recognise this principle when we say that preaching, in order to save the world, must be backed up by genuine Christian living. From reality to symbol, then, is a general principle of race education.

85. From Thing to Symbol is the Natural Order of the Mind. It is also a basic principle in the ducation of each child. Not only do the senses develop in advance of the reflectve powers, so that the first knowledge to be acquired is sense-knowledge, but this order represents a general principle of mental acquisition and growth. Not that all realities are sensible things, but simply that realities, as recognised in some kind of experience, come first, and the name, the formula, the theory comes afterward. A baby in the act of exploring one hand with the other, or handling every possible thing; a child who runs and jumps and climbs and tries to do whatever he sees anyone else doing; a boy who is possessed by an impulse to make bows and arrows, or toy wind mills; a youth who begins to hear the wide world whispering to him of a wider experience; a geologist, breaking a fragment from an exposed rock—all these illustrate the same great fact. The baby is laying up a stock of experiences which by and by he will learn to name. The child is learning nature's laws by bumping up against nature. The boy is expanding his insight by using upon things what insight he already has. The youth craves to get at the reality of life, and no mere telling him about life will suffice. In each of these cases the symbol, rule, or theory, when it comes, will have force and vitality in proportion to the felt reality of the experience for which it stands.

86. Significance of the Laboratory and of Manual Training. The contrast between the order of nature and traditional school methods is obvious enough. The traditional school is an institution that undertakes to transfer the contents of a text-book to the memory of the pupil. Yet a text-book is a lifeless, external thing; it is not a god to be bowed down to; it is not even the thing that the child has to learn. What has to be learned is the fact or the truth. The relation of a book to a fact or truth is like that of a window to a landscape. The window isn't the landscape; it doesn't contain the landscape; it is merely an opening through which

we may look for ourselves. Grammar, arithmetic, geography—these are not books, nor
are they contained in books, and no pupil is
really trained in them who does not resort
to the same sources as the book-makers themselves. The newer school-ideals, accordingly,
aim to bring the pupil into immediate touch
with the very things that the text-book talks
about. Hence the rapid spread of laboratories and manual training. By such means
the pupil not only secures opportunity for
self-activity; he also comes at the symbol
through the thing symbolised. He comes to
understand a generalisation by actual dealing
with some of the particulars upon which it
is based. He proves few things, of course,
and discovers less, but he becomes acquainted
with the methods of discovery and of proof,
and he acquires some experience of typical
facts and processes. Laboratories and manual training are purposely classed together in
this statement. Naturally, yet unfortunately,
the public has not discriminated adequately
between industrial training and manual training. The one has in view the learning of a
trade or art; the other broad general education. Manual training is not even, as its
name indicates, a training of the hands alone

or chiefly, but rather a training of the personality through the use of the hands and the mind at the same time.

87. Incomplete Applications of the Principle. The general principle, then, is that the symbol (name, formula, rule, theory) should enter only when the pupil already needs it in order to fix and formulate and generalise something with which he is already at least partially acquainted. This principle is easily misapplied. For example, the proper use of pictures is easily misunderstood. A true picture is, indeed, one degree nearer concreteness than mere words, yet pictures themselves are at best symbols. They, as well as words, have to be interpreted by the child's own experience. "Mother," said a little boy, "don't men ever go to heaven?" "Why do you ask?" replied the mother. "Because," said the little investigator, "none of the angels I have seen pictures of have whiskers!" It would be interesting to know what the gaudily colored pictures used weekly to illustrate the Sunday-school lesson in primary departments really mean to little children, and especially how far they really illustrate the lessons.

Another imperfect application of the

true principle is found in what used to be called "object lessons." For here the object placed before the child is commonly not the thing that is to be studied, but only a symbol for it, and often a very remote symbol, too. In the teaching of morals, physical analogues (a twig for the pliability of childhood, a tree for the fixation of maturity, etc.) may sometimes be a helpful addition to mere words, but at the best they merely improve our symbols. Even when the very object that the child has to study is placed before him, object teaching does not always succeed. When natural history, for example, is taught merely by means of museum specimens, the object, being exhibited out of its natural setting, and with none of the motion and "go" of nature, is never fully real to the pupil. Museum specimens, taken by themselves, tend to become only another kind of symbol. For this reason the pupil is to be taken into the field, where he beholds the life and movement of things, and is drawn out to take part in it himself.

Then comes the need of the symbol as a means of fixing, recalling, communicating what he has done and experienced. History, of course, has to be learned largely through analogues and symbols, yet now and then there is opportunity to exhibit some object actually connected with an historical event, and always our own institutions stand as monuments of the past. In general, dates, lists of kings, and similar abstract material should be withheld until they acquire meaning from something that already lives in the imagination. The story, historical and geographical pictures, the making of maps and diagrams, or dramatic representations, should come first. Many an adult can recall how dry and fruitless the study of history was until the reading of a biography or an historical romance, a visit to a battle field, the sight of an old flint-lock musket, or some similar event made history suddenly a living and moving reality.

88. Defects of the Catechetical Method. The application of this principle is perhaps more difficult in the teaching of moral and spiritual truth than anywhere else. For where shall the child experience the concrete fact? He can see and touch many of the things with which the state schools deal, but he has no similar sense-experience of God, or of Christ, or of duty. A large part of the task that will be undertaken in Part III consists in attempting to answer this question. Meantime we may well illustrate the prin-

ciple by one or two specific examples drawn
from the field of religious education. The
most obvious one is the method of catechetics.
The cathechetical instruction of the early
church was in close relation to reality, for it
was used as a means of preparing converts
from heathenism for formal admission into
the church. The convert already felt the new
life as a fact of experience; he then went on
through cathechetical study to formulate it
and try to understand it. This was catechetics in its original form. The instruction
of children by means of fixed questions and
answers is an entirely different thing. For
now the symbol is separate from the thing
symbolised, and an effort is made to fill the
child's memory with formulas the meaning of
which he cannot know in any vital way. These
formulas are expected to become useful by
and by. The mind is supposed to be pre-
empted by Christian truth and fortified
against the assaults of doubt. But the mind
is not really filled with truth. To communicate truth, as distinguished from symbols, implies assimilation of the truth through some
experience; it implies a vital, not mechanical,
reaction of the mind. Mere mechanical cate-
chising produces various results. Some

pupils merely shed the shower that falls upon them; they repeat the words and then forget them. Others, because the need of self-expression is ignored, feel themselves repressed, and therefore they become cynical or sceptical. Still others, filling their memory with forms of doctrine, assume that they have the truth, and so they become dogmatic or priggish. The very first condition for the success of a catechism is that the pupil should need a formula in which to express and generalise something that is already vital in his experience.[1]

89. Memorising Scripture. The memorising of Scripture is most useful when it obeys the principle, First the reality, then the symbol. Forcing upon the child the memorising of passages that lack the "tang" of reality to him may easily create prejudice against the whole Bible. The only safe plan, and the only one that is truly educative, is to see to it that the passage to be memorised conveys to the child a genuine meaning in which he has an interest of his own. Now, one of the best things about the form in which the Bible pre-

[1] Several recent catechisms seek to conform to pedagogical principles. See those by W. J. Mutch, New Haven, Conn.; those by J. L. Keedy, Lysander, N. Y.; Doremus Scudder's "Our Children for Christ" (Revell); W. E. McLennan's "The Lord's Supper (Eaton & Mains).

sents truth to us is that it is so concrete. It
is full of movement, and much of it has im-
perishable value simply as literary art. It
appeals at once to the imagination of a child
and the taste of a man. Further, the contents
of many parts of the Scriptures grow in
meaning as we ourselves grow. Of course we
have to wait for maturity before we realise
anything like their full depth, but there is
abundant reason why we should know them
as soon as they can begin to be genuine nutriment. The Twenty-third Psalm has a real
and natural application to childhood's interests, but the application grows more and more
profound with the moving years until old age
beholds itself descending into the valley of
deep darkness. The same is true of a large
proportion of the Scripture passages that
have endeared themselves to the hearts of
men throughout the ages. They can be understood by a child, though they cannot be
fully understood until the measure of life
has been filled to the brim. Happy the man
whose memory is stored with truth in the
forms of Biblical phraseology, for he has constant means of self-expression, and therefore
of self-understanding. The mere possession
of an appropriate symbol hastens the recogni-

tion of deeper reality. But the symbol must be really possessed; it must already be a symbol *of* something if its capacity for symbolising is to develop. Clearly, then, such passages as can have little or no meaning for a child should not be forcibly clamped upon his memory. Fortunately, near the end of childhood and the beginning of adolescence there develops great capacity and liking for memorising. At this time no hardship is felt in conning anything that is significant in matter and pleasing in form. By this time, too, the range of interest and the depth of moral appreciation have begun greatly to increase. This, then, is a peculiarly favorable period for storing the mind with the greatest words.

90. Some Cases in Point. Sense before sound! might well be the motto of every parent and teacher who undertakes to assist a child to memorize. Sully tells of a child who offered the first petition of the Lord's Prayer in the form, "Harold be thy name!" Here the sound is mis-heard, and consequently sense is entirely lacking. In other cases both sound and sense are misunderstood. A child upon returning home from Sunday school asked his mother, "Mamma, why should children bjthe their parents?"

Upon inquiry as to why the question was asked, the mother was informed that the pupils of the Sunday school had been taught this momentous command: "Children, *bathe* your parents in the Lord, for this is right!" Sometimes the words are understood, but the sense and application are distorted. Sully relates that one child, having heard the story of how the Good Samaritan poured oil into the wounds of the man who fell among thieves, understood that the Samaritan poured *paraffin* over the poor fellow![1] Another little boy who had recently heard the story of the creation of Eve came to his mother saying, "Mamma, I'm 'fraid I'm going to have a wife, for there's a drefful pain in my side!" If we could only know what meaning the children find in words and sentences, what a revelation we should have!

91. Making the "Application" in Bible Teaching. A notion has somehow grown up, probably through unconscious imitation of preaching, that the Bible is not really taught unless the "application" is stated. The biblical passage is first unfolded, and then, out of the teacher's own mind, or out of the mind

[1] James Sully: Studies of Childhood (New York, 1900), page 184. "Harold be thy name" will be found on p. 185.

of some editor of Sunday-school helps, there is brought forth something more which is supposed to form a climax. The aim that inspires this method is a true one, namely, the development of actual, present spiritual life in the pupil. But is the method adapted to the purpose in view? Life develops, not from symbol to experience, but from experience to symbol. What is actually done in this process of drawing out the "lesson" of the lesson is to increase the number of symbols without increasing the experience of reality. Generally, too, the process consists in following a strong symbol by a weaker one. Why should the Bible have the supreme place in the spiritual culture of the young? Because morals and religion are there presented better than we can present them in any words that we can form. Its strength lies, in part, in its freedom from abstract formulas, its nearness to the concrete, its self-revealing application to our own selves. Why, then, should a teacher feel called upon to add another and a weaker symbol to those of the sacred writings?

Suppose, for instance, that a Sunday-school teacher draws out of the lesson for the day the proposition, "We should be kind to one

another.'' This presupposes that the lesson
of kindness is actually embedded in the scripture passage. As soon as the pupil leaves the
class, or even before, he is likely to be confronted with a concrete opportunity to be
kind. What, now, has he gotten from the lesson that will induce him to be kind? The
least effective of all that he has gotten is the
teacher's formula; much more effective is the
passage of Scripture with its concrete picture; most effective of all will be the concrete,
scriptural kindness which the pupil has witnessed and experienced on the part of the
teacher. The influence is in proportion to the
concreteness of the material.

This principle does not imply reticence regarding spiritual truth, but rather that the
teacher should teach the Bible so well that the
pupil shall see for himself the spiritual truth
therein. Again, the principle does not forbid
making a direct appeal to the conscience of
the pupil on any fitting occasion. A ''fitting
occasion,'' however, is one in which some concrete reality—whether the teacher's personality, an historical incident, or the pupil's
own experience—overflows the spoken word
and makes it an instrument of reality.[1]

[1] *Cf.* Burton and Mathews: Principles and Ideals for
the Sunday School (Chicago, 1903), pages 100, 101.

92. Symbols apart from Reality Weaken Character. But this is not the end of the matter. We must ask not merely which is the stronger incitement to kindness, but also what is the effect of using weak incitements. Anyone who has studied the young can answer this question. The weakness of the symbol tends to be attributed to the thing symbolised. The anti-climax of the teacher's remarks about kindness tend to weaken respect for this virtue. Kindness comes to be associated in thought with weakness, and so manliness comes to signify some amount of roughness or disregard for others. Parallel results follow from teaching any other duty or any spiritual privilege in this way. The separation of the symbol from the thing symbolised results in the separation of thought from action; this implies action from impulse while principle looks on; but when principle becomes an onlooker instead of combatant, then character is left to chance. This is true of docile pupils as well as of restless and intractable ones. The docile pupil is likely to be simply a two or more sided one who reserves a part of his self-expression for other occasions. Or he may be unnaturally passive and compliant. In either case the

actual character fails to receive its proper
nutriment.   Character grows through reactions upon concrete facts and conditions.

93. Development of Character through Self-Adjustment to Community Life.
Specifically, what con-
crete facts and conditions?
Where is the child or the
youth to behold religion in
the concrete?   What is it
that is to stir him to action and awaken his
consciousness of principles?   In a word, the
kingdom of God actualised in various forms
of community life.   The family is, or should
be, the first form in which the kingdom con-
fronts the child.   Then come the public school
and the Sunday school.   In neither of these
is the chief task that of imparting information, but that of maintaining sound community life and carrying forward appropriate
community tasks.   Just as far as genuine
community life is maintained in either form
of school, the principles of the kingdom are
in actual operation.   The same principle is
found in other forms of human organisation,
and finally in the church.   Here is religion
objectively realised, and to it the child has to
adjust himself.   Through them he is to discover that he is a social being, that he has certain duties, and that the ultimate meaning of

life is found in that complete society in which
God loves us, and we love him and one another.[1] In a nutshell, then, the essential
method whereby reality is to be put before
symbol in religious education consists in placing such a social environment about the child
that his self-adjustments to it shall involve
both good habits and growing spiritual insight. In such an environment the Bible or
other symbols of religious life receive living
interpretation as, in turn, they illuminate the
facts and lead the way to higher things.

94. Necessity of the Symbol. Having laid much stress
upon the secondary place
of the symbol as compared with the experience that it registers, we must now remind
ourselves that our principle is not merely that
reality comes before symbol, but also that
symbol comes after reality. One of the most
important acquisitions of the human mind is
language. The naming of a thing is, in fact,
a part of the process of knowing it. The
name points out the qualities and relations of
a thing, and classifies it with other like things.

[1] One night a little child who had been accustomed to
use the prayer, "Now I lay me," requested permission to
make up a prayer of his own. Permission being given,
he prayed as follows: "O God, isn't it nice to ride in
the cable car! Please send me a bicycle. Amen."
Note the sense of fellowship, evidently a direct product
of human fellowships.

The name abides when the thing is absent; it can be called up by our own act, and can then take the mental place of the thing itself; by means of it we can communicate with one another, and even adjust our conduct to facts that are distant or future. This is possibly one reason why some early peoples believed that to know the name of a thing is to possess power over the thing itself. To let the members of another tribe know the name of one's tribal god, or even the real name of one's self was looked upon as dangerous. We must, indeed, put things first, but we must put symbols second. After a child has grasped an arithmetical or grammatical principle, the statement of it becomes a help in many ways. Definition helps clear thinking, and clear thinking helps toward wise self-control. The name, the rule, and finally the theoretical formula, all have a place in ethics and religion. As religious training has in the past erred by putting symbol in the place of reality, so there is danger in our days of not registering our moral and religious experience in any sufficient manner. Without definite registering of ideas communication becomes indefinite, and education ends either in sentimentality or in mechanical habit. In proportion, then, as the child mind, through its own concrete life, grows in ability to understand the symbols that express the truth to us, these symbols should be imparted.

CHAPTER XI

95. Character is Formed Partly through Suggestion and Imitation. We have just concluded that the chief factor in the development of character is found in the relations of the young to the various communities of which they are parts. Personality in its social aspects thus acquires first-class significance as an educational force. It is to be assumed, of course, that each community to which a child belongs, whether the family-community or any other, will prescribe some kind of rules to all its members, the children included, and that these rules will be enforced under the principle of self-expression as explained in Chapter IX. But this formulated element in the child's personal and social relations is by no means the only, or even the most influential one. There is in addition what goes under the name of "the influence of personality," and also what we might call "the influence of social atmosphere."

The present chapter will attempt an analy-

sis of these subtle influences. We cannot begin the analysis better than by a word concerning the psychological process by which
they become effective. The central features
of the process are called suggestion and imitation. The law of suggestion is that any
idea of an act or function tends to produce
that very act or function. For example, the
sight of a highly polished surface suggests to
us (very likely without our stopping to think
about it at all) the pleasant "feel" of such a
surface when the hand moves over it; consequently we tend (often without realising
what we are doing) to stroke such surfaces.
In the course of a minute or so I saw five
persons thus "feel" the marble wainscoting
as they moved down one of the corridors of
the Chicago Public Library. Suggestion can
come in un-numbered forms; it can come in
the language of advice or persuasion; it can
come in the acts which we see others perform;
it can come through our own inferences from
what we see or hear; even our own acts tend
to repeat themselves. The last is self-imita-
tion, and in general imitation operates
through suggestion. Deliberate imitation is
comparatively rare, while imitation of the sug-
gestive order is universal and constant. One

takes on the fashions or "fads" of the time,
the manners of one's social group, even the
language, tone of voice, and facial expression
of those with whom one is constantly associated, and all without clearly intending to
do so.

A moment's consideration of such facts
will show that this process is not a merely external one. We do not merely "take on" the
external aspects of what we imitate, but the
internal aspects also. We experience feelings
appropriate to the acts performed, and much
of this feeling apparently results from per-
forming the act. If the people all about us
on the street are walking fast, we quicken our
pace, and presently we feel hurried. It is
thus that mobs and panics exercise their mysterious control over individuals. Now, children are the greatest imitators, and thereby
they form not only external habits, but also
habitual modes of feeling, thinking, and as-
piring—in a word, character.

96. The Influence of Personality. Apart from all our intentions, then, and even
against our intentions, personality propagates
itself. More than anything else, education in
its initial stages is the propagation of character through imitation working by sugges-

tion. In the long run, what the teacher or the parent gives to the young is just one's self, very little more and very little less. What one is in both mental and bodily habit is transmitted either by means of method or in spite of it. A nervous teacher will have nervous pupils; a peevish or arbitrary parent will have peevish or arbitrary children. The child will adopt the political and religious opinions of parent and teacher without argument; he will accept their standard of right and wrong. Thus it is that a strong and wholesome personality may counteract defective methods, while the best of methods never succeeds in the absence of such personality. Of course, the highest result is to be reached only when the best personal qualities are joined with right choice of material and the best methods of using it.

97. "Condescending" to Children and Youth. The personal element in teaching is what we really are. It is not something that can be put on when we are with the young and taken off when we are away from them. Anything merely put on tends to defeat its own aim. The young have sharp eyes and what they do not distinctly see they often feel. To put into the voice a

tone, or into the face a look, or into our acts
a manner that we do not really feel is to run
great risk of creating a suspicion that we are
not quite genuine. Who can measure the
amount of repugnance toward the church that
has been awakened by the professional tone
that is often assumed by religious workers?
The professional tone is a sign that a fence
has been built around one's personality. It
means that a man is giving to his fellows
things or ideas, but not himself. How many
times has a spontaneous laugh knitted together teacher and pupil by revealing the real
man or woman in the teacher! The pupil discovers spiritual kinship between himself and
the teacher who laughs with him, for the two
partake of a common experience.[1] This is a
typical case, and it stands for the general
truth that the positive influence of personality grows out of the sharing of experience,
whereby all the processes of suggestion, imitation, sympathy, and self-expression become
free.

On the other hand, a negative or repulsive
influence of personality arises when one per-

[1] "Seldom should smiling, never laughing, have place
in religious instruction," says A. Vinet.—Pastoral
Theology (New York, 1856), page 234. To take this
ground is to lessen the human touch through which alone
the best that is in the teacher reaches the child.

son seeks to influence or control another without sharing his actual experience. Thus offers of mere pity are often resented just when sympathy is most needed. We do not wish to be merely pitied, but we do long for companionship. A faithful dog that shares our bad fortune with us can comfort us more than a man who merely reaches an arm down to help us. The same principle appears in the vanity of giving alms without love, and of trying to do by means of money and institutions what only the sharing of life can ever accomplish. "Come, let us live with our children," said Froebel. No educational machinery can ever take the place of this living with the young, this entrance as a sincere partner into their experience, and the corresponding admission of them as real partners into one's mature interests.

98. Childlikeness in Men and Women. But how can a mature person return to a level of life that he has long left behind? And how can a child be a real partner in mature interests? Must not the common plane upon which maturity meets childhood be simulated? The answer is that a normally developed manhood or womanhood retains something of childlikeness within it-

self. That we lose the child-heart and the
child-mind out of us results from false education and from our sin and folly. The greatest
characters have ever retained the child within
themselves, so that the perennial wonder of
the populace is that its heroes are so simple,
so spontaneous, so much ''like one of the family.'' The truly great man is nearer to the
common people and nearer to childhood than
those would-be great men who dry and shrink
and stiffen in the heat of artificial ambitions.
What we need, then, is not condescension to
the young, but rather rediscovery of the perennial springs of our own childhood. Play, for
example, should never cease to be a part of
our daily routine, and even the simplest plays
should retain a native interest for us. We
would be better, happier, more efficient men
if we took a larger part with children in tag,
or hide-and-seek, or marbles and jackstones,
or kite-flying, or ball playing; and, sharing
thus in the experiences of the young, we
should have a far larger influence over them.

99. Letting the Young Share in Mature Interests. On the other hand, it is
possible to admit the young
at an early age to genuine
participation in the occupations or daily
duties of their elders. Children long for oppor-

tunities to do things. They watch their elders
at work and wish for some part to do. What
a boon it is when some sympathetic person
permits even a little co-operation. A little
girl would rather have some part in the house-
keeping than not; a little boy is never happier
than when the father permits him to fetch
and carry, to handle tools, to feed or drive
the domestic animals, provided, always, that
such occupation brings real companionship
with the parent in accomplishing something.
Here is one point at which country boys have
the advantage of city boys. In the country
the family performs more kinds of service for
itself, so that there is a larger variety of possible occupations for the boy as well as his
father. The first time that a farmer's boy is
permitted to take a horse to the blacksmith
shop all by himself is likely never to be forgotten. The first time that any boy is trusted
to carry a package of money or to perform
some other act of real importance his sense of
responsibility and of honor is likely to burst
into sudden blossom. He feels himself to be
a part of the real world, and to be bound by
strong ties to his parents and their standards.
Such touches of reality can begin very early in
life, and they can be graded to fit the child's

growing capacity. They develop the habit of living a real life, that is, a life of social responsibility as contrasted with mere caprice or mere impulse; and this habit of living in realities goes farther toward developing solid character than rivers of mere instruction and advice. Moral instruction, in fact, becomes significant only in proportion as it has some such background, or rather in proportion as it is an integral part of living in the realities of life. Knowing the right and doing the right need to be fused into one.

Thus, after all, the one prime essential for moral and religious education is that the young should live a common life with moral and religious elders. A common life: this does not mean living under the same roof, or eating from the same table, or receiving commands and advice; it means having experiences and occupations in common, so that the real self of each, with its actual interests, is revealed freely to the other. This law applies, too, not merely to the externals of conduct or to mere morals; it reaches to the inner recesses of the soul. A child who lives in such relations as these with elders who are vitally spiritual comes in the most natural way to include spirituality in his notion of real life;

he takes it for granted; it becomes his law, and he makes efforts to obey it just as spontaneously as he makes effort to win his games.

100. Fellowship the Starting Point of Both Good and Evil Character. If we trace any character, good or bad, to its sources, we always find it starting in fellowship. The young life comes into contact with a wholesome or unwholesome personality, and catches its spirit as if by infection. From the idle gossip of neighbors to the revelry of a saloon, the entering wedge of evil is fellowship. Remove this element, and the remaining factors in temptation of many kinds would appear so gross as to lose much of their attractiveness, at least to one who is taking the first steps in evil. After a sinful habit of any kind is set up, to be sure, coarser and coarser motives suffice. But the point at which the first step is taken is not solicitation by any coarse motive in its native coarseness, but in the garb of good fellowship, conformity to custom, amiable compliance with the standards of other persons. In the pleasant atmosphere of fellowship, all the forces of imitation and suggestion work unimpeded upon an unformed character to give it the complexion of its surroundings. We do not become either good or evil, either

religious or irreligious, merely by deliberate
choice, and any plan of moral and religious
education that depends for success primarily
and chiefly upon such choices is sure to let go
the golden opportunity. The great lever of
good, as of evil, is fellowship, the sharing of
life.

101. The Mixed Environment of the Young, and our Resulting Duty. Theoretically the problem
of moral and religious edu-
cation is not particularly
formidable. Keep the child
in constant fellowship with Christian character and away from all other character, let instruction keep pace with the growing powers,
and the work is done. But the practical problem is not as simple as this. For the actual
environment of every child is mixed. In us
who follow Christ the wheat and the chaff are
not yet separated, and among the persons with
whom the child is in touch many are not dis-
ciples. We simply cannot shut up any child
to an environment that is completely wholesome; we cannot shut out temptation and the
liability of a fall. Even if we could compass
such a plan, children subjected to it would
not be prepared for life in a world like ours.
They would not understand the world or their
own place in it. Rightly understood, the child-

hood of Jesus, his bringing up in a social environment made up of both evil and good, is
an essential feature of the incarnation. Terri-
ble as the danger is, the very best thing for
the child is that he should be subjected to the
evil as well as the good influences of his social
environment. Only so come discrimination,
strength of resistance, realisation of the
world's need, practical adaptation, and the
soldierly spirit in the contest for the kingdom
of God. But, this being the case, the duty is
upon us to make of religious and moral education a never-sleeping, never-pausing campaign. We are not merely to extend information and advice to the young; nay, we are to
fight evil in the concrete side by side with the
child. The chief feature of the schooling of
his character is to be his participation in our
work and in our fight to set up the kingdom
of God in the world.

The strategic position in the campaign of
moral and religious education now becomes
plain. It is the element of fellowship. We are
to make wholesome fellowships—whether in
the home, the school, the church, the college,
or the neighborhood—so warm, so natural, so
unremitting, so unreserved that every unwholesome fellowship shall seem artificial and

Our problem, then, is simply this: How can the relatively passive impressions of childhood become a genuine factor in personal reflection and choice except under the inertia of mere habit? The solution of the problem is to be found in providing the child with presuppositions that have the simplicity, the directness, the appealing eloquence of the eternally and obviously real. What the youth most needs when he comes to the age of self-questioning is to feel that his life is already real, not artificial. He feels this with respect to affection between himself and his parents, and consequently, in spite of the chafings under parental authority, in spite of the acts of rebellion, that come into the life of most youths, very rarely do the youth's feelings really cut loose from the family. There remains a fundamental sense of reality. This is the heart of the problem of moral and religious training—to be real, to rely upon nothing artificial, to bring the eternal into the forms of a child's daily life, and into the forms of a child's daily thought. The youth will receive some help from reasoned instruction; he will receive more from a continuance of that sharing of life of which mention has been made; he will be greatly in-

individual variations by the sheer force of training received while the personality was passively compliant. This is substantially the method in use by the Catholic church. It, too, fails to give scope to the principle of free self-activity. It thinks of the teaching authority as one that not merely feeds but also commands the intellect, even prescribing pains and penalties for variations. This is simply a modified form of the theory of compulsion, for to prevent the individual will from becoming conscious of itself is to compel the personality just as truly as to crush a will that has once become self-conscious.

106. How Prevent a Break with Childhood Training? The third theory encourages the full blossoming of self-conscious thought and self-conscious will, even though this brings peril of false thinking and wrong choices. It declares that there is no other way in which the personality can become fully mature. The danger of this theory is that it shall rely too much upon a single phase of what ought to be a continuous process. Certainly we should not expect adolescence to be a completely new beginning; neither conversion nor any other process ever makes up for the neglect of early training.

forced. It is a distinctly wholesome sign for
a child up to the beginning of adolescence
simply to assume that he is included with his
parents within the kingdom of God, and to
take no thought for decisions or experiences
other than those directly involved in filling his
proper place in the family, in the school,
among his playmates, etc. During this period,
therefore, the character is forming chiefly under the silent and unconscious influence of the
personal and social environment. But, suddenly or gradually, the child awakens into a
self-conscious, self-acting, factor in the formation of his own character.

**105. The Will not
to be Suppressed
by Compulsion or
Authority.** There are three theories
as to what is now to be
done for him. The first
theory advises simple com-
pulsion: Compel the youth to go to church,
to read his Bible, to pray, to learn
his catechism; repress his doubts by stern
condemnation; in a word, choose for him.
This would, of course, violate the entire theory
of development through free self-activity. The
second theory advises that reliance be placed
upon habit and standard already formed. The
idea is to keep the youth going through the
same motions as in childhood, and to prevent

Christ from the start, just as he counts himself an American or a member of his father's family.

104. But Self-Conscious Choice Must Come. While it is true that personality is "catching," and that much of the best work in character training is effected through imitation and suggestion, it is also true that character depends upon deliberate choices. We cannot rely upon the force of mere imitation or suggestion to carry anyone through the crises of moral and spiritual experience. There will arise the insistent question whether the habitual presupposition is correct, and also that ofttimes tragical question, what kind of success one shall choose to seek, what kind of self one shall choose to be. What, now, is the relation of the personal and social forces that we have described to the voluntary factor that now enters into the problem? The problem of personal choices does not normally grow acute until the beginning or middle of adolescence, that is, not much before the years from twelve to fifteen, though it may arise in minor and gradually increasing degree before that age. This self-conscious element in moral and spiritual development should be permitted to awaken spontaneously. It should not be

fluenced by the mere habits of his childhood;
but that which will hold him most firmly and
certainly to conservative choices will be his
immediate feeling of the naturalness and
reality of his existing standards.

PART II
THE CHILD